AF576657

Thank You for Hearing My Call

Living the Messages of Medjugorje

by

Rev. Gerald P. Ruane & Ruthann Williams, op

Sacred Heart Press
Caldwell, NJ

 Published in the United States by Sacred Heart Press, Caldwell, New Jersey.

ISBN 1-56237-002-2

Sacred Heart Press
Suite 5C
585 Bloomfield Avenue
Caldwell, NJ 07006

201-226-7077

Dedication

You are our mother.
We answer your call
to pray with our hearts
for salvation of all.

Beautiful Lady,
you teach us to love.
You lead us to Jesus
and the Father above.

On the Institute pilgrimage to Medjugorje from November 6-13, 1990, we asked Vicka to bring this manuscript to her daily meeting with our Lady. She graciously did so, and returned the manuscript with this lovely note.

Dear Friends,

May the Queen of Peace bless you with her love and give you much joy so that you can persevere on your way.

Truly from my heart I greet you. I pray for you and carry you in my heart.

Yours,
Vicka

Sister Ruthann, the visionary Vicka, and Father Ruane in Medjugorje, November 10, 1990.

Acknowledgements

With grateful hearts we acknowledge all those who encouraged, supported and assisted us during the writing of this book.

Special thanks are due to Ed and Agnes Kardauskas, Elenore Manger, Rosalie Miserendino, Frances Peterson, Marie Gatza and Robert Suszko.

Finally, we want to thank Fathers Slavko and Phillip and the other priests, sisters, and people of Saint James parish in Medjugorje.

Photo Credits

Roger and Carey Ann Caswell
front cover

Rosemary Hegemiller
pages 179, 184

Linn Neandross
pages 66, 86, 121

Robert Suszko
pages 31, 53, 74, 113, 126, 160

Frances Toohey
pages 142, 174

Contents

St. James Church is the parish church of Medjugorje. The apparitions take place in a room in the tower on the left, just off the choir loft.

The site of the early apparitions, Apparition Hill, is located at Bijakovici near Medjugorje.

The Mountain of the Cross is called Mt. Krizevac. The cross, which dominates the valley, was erected in 1933 on the 1900th anniversary of our Lord's Resurrection.

Introduction

It was our original intention to write this book for those who had been to Medjugorje, to help them live out that experience. But our Lady calls us to share the messages, to spread the word, to let our light shine before all. So as we wrote and prayed and talked together, it became clear that our approach should be enlarged and that **Thank You for Hearing My Call** *should be written for all God's people.*

If you have been to Medjugorje, there will be much here that is familiar to you. Rejoice in that gift.

If you have not been there, know that Mary's call is no less intended for you. You need not climb Mt. Krizevac (the Mountain of the Cross) to experience the cross. You need not attend Mass at Saint James (the parish church of Medjugorje) to know the healing love of our Eucharistic Lord. Nor need you stand on Apparition Hill (the place where our Lady first appeared to the visionaries) to hear Mary's words.

The experience of Medjugorje is an experience of the heart, available to all who love the Lord. So long as you open your heart to the movement of God within you, so long as you are attentive to Mary's Gospel-based messages, you can "live" Medjugorje.

And she will say to all of us, "Thank you for hearing my call."

We want to echo that sentiment most sincerely as you begin to read this book.

Father Ruane and Sister Ruthann

A Note About the Type

This book speaks in four voices: our Lady's, ours jointly, and ours individually. In order to help you distinguish among them, you will find that as the voice changes, so does the style of type which is being used.

When we speak together, it will appear in this type style.

When I (Father Ruane) speak, the type used will be this one.

When I (Sister Ruthann) speak, the type will look like this.

Our Lady's words will appear in a type to match whichever of us is speaking. Her words will always be set off in quotation marks.

PART 1

Dear children
I invite you
to live in God's love.
Abandon yourselves
to his will.
You can be holy
and perfect within.

Thank you
for hearing my call.

PART 1

Beginnings

This book started out as one person's view of how to live the messages of Medjugorje. A friend of mine suggested I (Father Ruane) write a book about the healings that occur at Medjugorje and especially about appropriating them (claiming, owning, and enjoying them) on one's return home.

I readily agreed to the suggestion and began to put some ideas on paper. However, I soon discovered that there was so much more than healing to write about with regard to Medjugorje. Healings there were aplenty, but they had to be fitted into the larger picture of Medjugorje.

As I expanded the scope of the book, Sister Ruthann shared some of her own unique insights and offered to help. Thus the book became not one person's view, but two people's sharing their insights from their individual and quite different perspectives. We are quite different in many ways and attitudes, gifts and backgrounds. Because of that we make a good team as God helps us to achieve a common purpose and approach. I believe that has made this a much better work.

Just as we were finishing up the first draft I began to experience tremendous pressure whenever I tried to write. From June 13 to August 13 I experienced a time of testing, distractions, and temptations. It was a case of writer's block, and even more than that. I now see it as the devil's effort to prevent this book from being finished. And yet, during all that period, the call was never far from my mind and heart. Finally on August 13 (within reach of our Lady's feast day honoring her Assumption into heavenly glory), I felt at peace once again. Our Lady of Peace (her title at Medjugorje) brought me safely through all the trials and gave me great peace and the assurance needed to go forward with this work.

I am writing this on the Assumption, and I know the power and love of our Lady's intercession for me, Sister Ruthann, and all who have helped in the writing of **Thank You for Hearing My Call.** Through all the times of testing and temptation, one song has helped me immensely.

So let's begin this book of sharing by two people from New Jersey with the song of a third party from an entirely different locale: Hawaii. Medjugorje has a way of bringing together people from all over the world, and so often the experience of Medjugorje continues to bind them together after their return home.

Rejoice with me at the wonderful ways of God who has touched so many hearts throughout the United States and the whole world. Praise him now and forever.

Message From Our Lady
by Robin Leong

You are our Mother.
We answer your call
To pray with our hearts
For salvation of all.
Beautiful Lady,
You teach us to love.
You lead us to Jesus
And the Father above.

Dear children, I invite you
To pray with your hearts.
The Lord wants to cleanse you of sin.
You need my help; you can't do it alone.
Thank you for hearing my call.

You are our Mother.
We answer your call
To pray with our hearts
For salvation of all.
Beautiful Lady,
You teach us to love.
You lead us to Jesus
And the Father above.

Dear children, I invite you
To live in God's love.
Abandon yourselves to his will.
You can be holy and perfect within.
Thank you for hearing my call.

You are our Mother.
We answer your call
To pray with our hearts
For salvation of all.
Beautiful Lady,
You teach us to love.
You lead us to Jesus
And the Father above.

Dear children, I invite you
To pray for peace.
The world is in serious sin.
Kneel before the cross of our Lord Jesus Christ.
Thank you for hearing my call.

You are our Mother.
We answer your call
To pray with our hearts
For salvation of all.
Beautiful Lady,
You teach us to love.
You lead us to Jesus
And the Father above.

How beautifully this hymn summarizes our Lady's messages in their essentials. Please note well how Mary speaks. She calls us her dear children and then invites us to do something. Then she concludes by thanking us for responding to her call.

What a beautifully gentle and loving approach she uses. How respectful she is of our free will. She is pedagogically on target and yet the quintessential Mother. She understands our need to be free and responsible for our actions and yet she knows our limitations. That's why she repeats her invitation to pray and fast, to convert and to believe so often. She is always our Mother, lovingly consistent and gently insistent, but calmly persistent in the face of our failures to live the messages. Her loving and exquisitely gentle invitation touched me deep within my spirit in those two months when I experienced writer's block and the buffetings of temptations and oppression. Even when I slowed down and for a few days gave up praying and fasting as she had requested, I always knew she loved me. I could and did often say to her:

"You are my Mother.
Help me to answer your call . . .
Beautiful Lady,
please teach me to love
and lead me to Jesus
and the Father above."

I think I pay no better compliment to Robin Leong than to take his words and music and make them the basis for my personal prayer and praise.

Mary will never stop being our Mother. You can depend on her prayers as you read through this book. May she help you to read with heart and mind open to receive and answer her beautiful invitation to return to the Lord our God.

CHAPTER 1

I Believe!

I (Father Ruane) was blessed to be on sabbatical during 1989-90; and in the eight months from the beginning of November to the first week of June, I went to Medjugorje four times. Each pilgrimage was a blessed experience; each one was quite different.

The first time I went I was really completely unaware of the impact that Medjugorje would have on me. I went with some skepticism, yet with a relatively open mind, to see a renewed parish. I did see that, but I saw something more. I came back a believer, but I don't think I really appropriated the message. It did not become a part of my daily life.

In February I went for a personal retreat which was a blessing and moved me closer to acceptance, but not completely. I did begin praying all fifteen decades of the rosary and doing some of the other things our Lady recommended. I was giving out medals and rosaries from Medjugorje, but in some way I was still, especially with other priests, acting the cool, clerical, impartial observer. I wanted to protect my reputation and my self-respect. After all, I wouldn't want anyone to think I was a religious fanatic, would I?

After my third pilgrimage, I realized my mixed motives and it suddenly dawned on me that I truly believed that our Lady was appearing at Medjugorje. Whether every message was translated accurately, whatever the outcome of the dispute between the diocesan bishop and the Franciscans, I believe that our Lady is appearing there and that the messages are accurate to the largest extent.

Getting Off the Fence

So I had to get off the fence and stop trying to be "Chaplain Cool." I began to say: "I believe in the message and I want to live the message and I will live the message with God's help." My personality is the type that is analytical and in some ways distrustful of emotionalism, but I hope that I will never distrust emotions since they are God-given gifts, complementing the gifts of reason and intellect. And all three — emotion, reason, and intellect — were now speaking in unison about the truth and relevance of Medjugorje for our world.

I was ready personally to begin a serious living-out of the messages. But was it enough that I keep this to myself?

Although by then I had been to Medjugorje three times (and would return for Pentecost), I had never written anything about it. I had shared with several people and talked at two days of recollection, but I had not put anything on paper. Then I began to put some notes together because my friend had suggested very strongly that I write this book about my experiences. I decided to give it a try and to stress four things:

1. what to do upon returning to one's home;

2. how to live the messages;

3. the fruits of Medjugorje in one's life; and

4. appropriating and claiming the healings associated with Medjugorje.

The Bishop of Mostar

I made some notes, discussed the project with Sister Ruthann and others, but did not get down to the hard work of researching and writing. Then came the article from the Bishop of Mostar in the spring of 1990.

The article appeared in our Archdiocesan newspaper and was probably syndicated around the country. It explained that the Bishop of Mostar, in whose diocese Medjugorje is located, had just recently published a sixteen-page booklet. In it he denied the validity of the apparitions, claiming that they were a fraud perpetrated by the Franciscans to gain power and control over the people. The Bishop also said that, in his opinion, no matter what spiritual blessings resulted from the pilgrimages to Medjugorje, they just were not worth the fraud involved.

I had visions of people reading that article and accepting it as absolute truth. I did not agree with the Bishop's views. I knew something about the situation and had read a great deal more about the difficulties between the Bishop and the Franciscans in that Croatian province, difficulties which in some way were distracting people from the message of Medjugorje.

I would like to "begin" this book by presenting what I wrote as a result of reading about the Bishop of Mostar's opposition. An abbreviated version appeared in "The Catholic Advocate," the newspaper of the Roman Catholic Archdiocese of Newark, New Jersey. Please, read it over carefully. It will be, I hope, a good introduction to our book in which we will be developing many of the points I could only mention briefly in my response.

The Supreme Authority of Rome

We would also add, however, that in all things we submit to the authority of Rome. Only the Church can pass a final and definitive judgment on the events at Medjugorje. But such ecclesial investigations take time, while our Lady's messages have an urgency about them that needs to be heard and responded to now. They are the Gospel messages proclaimed and reiterated today to our world which seems to have forgotten them. Insofar as they echo the Gospel, they are a call to conversion and commitment which we dare not ignore.

A Priest's Reflection on Medjugorje

The recent article about the Bishop of Mostar's view of Medjugorje provides me with the opportunity to offer another view of the subject. But before I begin the major portion of what I have to say, I would invoke the intercession of our Lady of Medjugorje, the Queen of Peace, for all those involved in the dispute: the Bishop of Mostar, the priests and people of Saint James parish, the visionaries and their families, and all the pilgrims from all over the world whose hearts have heard the message of our Lady, but whose minds are troubled and confused by the argument. Holy Mother, bring the light of your Son to this situation and in his name and power, give us peace.

I had had some interest in going to Medjugorje and even had two opportunities in October of 1988. But the time was not right. However, the opportunities themselves piqued my curiosity and I began to read what I could find about the apparitions. Belief and skepticism fought a battle in my mind. I wanted to believe because it seemed that so many wonderful things were happening there. But I held back.

Visions and apparitions were not a part of my daily life. I had enough problems as a human, a Christian, a priest, and a pastor of a large parish. So I put it out of my mind, on a back burner somewhere. But every once in a while it would grab my attention as people who had been there came home changed and converted to a more deeply Christian way of life.

Then came a call to the Institute. Would I go as spiritual director for a group of pilgrims? Initially I was reluctant to accept as the plans for my year's sabbatical were not complete. I suggested that Sister Ruthann go as the spiritual director and only later decided to join the group. Thus the two of us were to be in Medjugorje in November of 1989 with forty-one other pilgrims.

I went with some reserve about the events at Medjugorje, but I did want to see a renewed parish, which is what I had heard Saint James in Medjugorje had become as a result of the apparitions. At that time one hundred Italian priests were there on retreat. (Actually that planted the thought in my mind that Medjugorje would be an ideal place for a retreat.)

On that first trip there was a great and almost endless opportunity to celebrate the Eucharist in a variety of languages each day. Eucharist was certainly the central focus of my first time there. Praying the rosary in church and many other places was another great experience of God's grace.

I returned home no longer doubting that something wonderful and very spiritual was occurring in Medjugorje. After that, I began to read more about the messages and found them to be basically the Gospel message of conversion, commitment to God, prayer, fasting, and peace. I knew I wanted to go back, but had no definite plan to do so.

Then a friend invited me to go with him in February. He knew how I had been changed by my first visit there (I didn't yet realize how much) and he suggested that I use the pilgrimage as a retreat time. Remembering the one hundred Italian priests who impressed me so much on my first trip, I jumped at that chance and went with a small group of people to whom it was abundantly clear why I was there.

The Eucharist was once again the focal point, but as there was only one other English speaking priest there, I had more opportunities to minister to people in the sacrament of Penance/Reconciliation. When I wasn't in church or celebrating the sacrament, I had time for quiet prayer, reading, reflection, and listening to the Lord. I was nourished in many ways by this time.

I was deeply impressed by the people who were there, the sacrifices they had made to get there and how their lives were touched by the Lord working through his Blessed Mother. For me, it was definitely a mountaintop experience. I returned home renewed and grateful for the Lord's gift to me of a second pilgrimage to Medjugorje.

The third time I went was to be with a group of seventy-five people from central Jersey who were going for Holy Week. The group was quite large and included many families. (There were ten children under twelve years of age and about eight teenagers and eight college-age students.) It was an inspiration to learn of the great sacrifices these families had made in order to be able to go together.

This time one of my three sisters and three of the volunteers from the Sacred Heart Institute came. Their reactions and enthusiasm, their conversations and conversions and prayers were powerful witnesses to me. Once again the Eucharist each day, in fact, twice a day — once in English and once in Croatian — and the rosary prayed with twelve to fifteen hundred people in the church were the highlights.

During this visit I had even greater opportunity to celebrate the sacrament of Penance/Reconciliation with people from all over the world, and I was amazed at what the Lord was doing in them through the words of his Mother.

On May 28 of 1990, I observed the 30th anniversary of my priestly ordination. On the 20th we had a celebration for my family, people from the Sacred Heart Institute and other friends. Early that morning I decided to go back to Medjugorje for Pentecost with another one of my sisters and her daughter, and some friends who would be celebrating their 30th wedding anniversary during our time there.

I have been deeply touched by my experiences at Medjugorje and have experienced a deepening of my prayer life and joy in my priesthood. Over twelve million people have gone to Medjugorje in the nine years since the apparitions began. The ones whom I know have been deeply touched, some more than others, as is always the case.

The fruits of Medjugorje have been good and have been plentiful. In the Archdiocese of Newark, New Jersey, there are several Medjugorje prayer groups that meet every week and a monthly Medjugorje peace Mass which packs the church where it is held. The Sacred Heart Institute has sponsored two afternoons of recollection on the message of Medjugorje. The crowds were not large, but at each one something special happened. In all cases, the fruits have been very blessed.

I have never known an apparition of our Lady to receive the media exposure that Medjugorje has. It has been examined in books, in magazines, in pamphlets, in audio and video cassettes, on national and international radio and television. (My niece, who came to Medjugorje in June, is writing a paper for her M.A. in journalism on the apparitions.) Many people initially went to Medjugorje to expose what was happening as a fraud, while others went with healthy doses of skepticism. They all came back believers.

Centers of Peace have sprung up all over the United States and throughout the world. They are places for information and provide books and audio and video tapes, etc. Some of them even arrange and escort pilgrimages to Medjugorje at quite reasonable cost.

The unfortunate feud between the Bishop of Mostar and the Franciscans of that particular province is to be deeply regretted. The Bishop was initially very supportive and enthusiastic about the apparitions and visited the parish about five times. The pastor at that time, Father Jozo, was quite skeptical and urged the Bishop to be more cautious in his endorsement of what was happening.

The Bishop turned against the apparitions when it was reported that our Lady was supporting the Franciscans whom he had censured. You may read a full account of this in Father Rene Laurentin's book **Messages and Teachings of Mary at Medjugorje** (The Riehle Foundation, Milford, Ohio, 1988, pp. 325-343).

Father Jozo, on the other hand, came to accept the validity of the apparitions after he had tested the six children very strenuously and after much prayer. He later was sentenced to jail by the government which was trying to stop the apparitions. He served eighteen months at hard labor before being released. He and the other Franciscans who have taken his place at Medjugorje impress me as people who are not perpetrating a fraud, but are doing the work of the Lord almost sixteen hours each day — nearly every day of the year.

I have great respect for the office of bishop in the Church (although as a student of Church history I do know how individual bishops have erred at times). My prayer once again and even daily is that Our Lady of Peace, the Mother of the Prince of Peace, will bring the divine healing of her Son to the situation between the Bishop and the Franciscans.

For I truly believe that Mary has appeared at Medjugorje and has touched many lives as a result. In fact, Sister Ruthann, myself, and many others see a direct link between the Medjugorje phenomenon of people being converted and praying and the recent overthrow of Communism in Eastern Europe.

In 1858 our Lady appeared at Lourdes. "Pray and be converted," she said. In 1917, she came once again, to Fatima. "Pray and be converted," she said. Since 1981 she has been visiting Medjugorje. "Pray, pray, pray and be converted," she says. At Lourdes she appeared in the morning, at Fatima in the afternoon, and at Medjugorje in the evening.

Is this the evening of the day that began in 1858?

Let us pray for truth. Let us pray for peace. Let us pray for conversion. Let us pray.

CHAPTER 2

Returning Home

The first time I (Father Ruane) left Medjugorje I had to go on to Rome for some appointments, so there was no question of prolonging my stay in Yugoslavia. The other three times I desperately wanted to stay for a few more hours, days, or a week in that lovely spot so dear to the Spirit and his Bride.

On my fourth pilgrimage (May 31 to June 7), I tried my best to stay an extra week but could not. I did, however, send the pilgrims off to Dubrovnik after the morning Mass, and gained five extra hours there before taking a taxi to Dubrovnik. It was worth the cost and the hair-raising experience of traveling around some spectacular turns in the road while the driver tried to show me pictures of his wife and children. My conversion experience, begun at Medjugorje, was deepened. He drove; I prayed and repented fervently (and often).

But back to my first pilgrimage when I was ready to leave for Rome. Before visiting the Eternal City I would have a two-day rest period in Dubrovnik. I was looking forward to that because I could finally get some time for quiet reflection on my experiences. I wasn't at Medjugorje physically, but I was there in every other dimension of my being.

A Gentle Leave-Taking

So my first departure from Medjugorje was a gentle and loving one. I knew I would miss the emphasis on prayer and fasting and that intense concentration on the Eucharist that had so touched me as a priest and as a pilgrim and as one who believes so strongly in the healing power of the Mass. But I felt reassured by the fact that our Lady would be with me. She had always been a part of my life and now she was much more at center stage than she had been for several years when I had slackened in my appreciation of her as mother, companion, and friend.

Did I want to return? Very much so and there was no denying that. When would I return? I had no idea, but I sincerely prayed that it would be soon. God heard that prayer and gave me not just one but three more chances to be a pilgrim to that lovely and blessed village where our Lady's presence continually calls us to follow her Son more faithfully each day.

Did I need to go back three times? I think so as each time deepened my appreciation of the messages and their application to my life. But I'm getting ahead of myself so let's just leave it at that first departure when I prayed that God would help me get back there as soon as possible.

* * * * * *

I Wanted to Stay

If I (Sister Ruthann) never in my life before understood Peter's reluctance to leave Mount Tabor, I understood it on the morning I knew I had to leave Medjugorje. I wanted to stay, caught up in the vision, held in the sacredness, timeless in time, and captured in prayer.

How could I leave so soon? I had arrived just a week before, an unbeliever. I had spent four and a half days still an unbeliever. Oh, I had prayed and gone to Mass, sometimes a couple of times a day. But I had missed so much. I hadn't gone to see Father Jozo. I hadn't heard any of the visionaries speak except for Ivan. While the others had spent two hours each evening in prayer and Eucharist at the church, I had opted to rest and relax for the evening ahead. Oh, yes, it had been time more or less well spent. But now it was time to go. I had been a believer only a day and a half! And in light of what I had come to believe, I knew the time could have been spent in so much better ways. (Lord, let me never waste another precious moment of my life.)

But the leave-taking day was upon me. The sun was not quite up when I literally ran across the fields to arrive, panting, at the foot of Apparition Hill. Did I have time to climb once more? No. I had come as close as I could to that holy place where the Mother of God had stood among her sons and daughters. I knelt at the foot of the path and prayed and cried. Oh, how I wanted to stay! How could I leave her, these people, this place of never-ending prayer? Why, after all my days of doubting, I'd only begun to explore Medjugorje with my heart! It was too soon to go, too soon.

"Oh, God," I prayed, "I can't leave here. I can't go back. It's too new. I'll lose it all. Please, Jesus. Please, Mary. Help me. This is too hard to do alone."

But it had to be. Reluctantly I returned to the house and the bus for Dubrovnik where I discovered the rest of the reluctant-to-leave pilgrims. In that community I found some consolation. But not enough. I hoped for a miracle, something that would intervene and keep us from leaving. Anything. But "anything" didn't happen. The sun didn't dance for me. My rosary stayed stubbornly silver. No lights flashed. No bells rang. The luggage was loaded. We climbed on board. The driver started the motor. Good-bye, Medjugorje. Good-bye. Good-bye.

On the bus I know we prayed the rosary and I know we listened to the tape "Beyond the Fields." And I know I put what I thought would be a permanent crick in my neck straining to look back as the towers of Saint James became smaller and smaller and finally disappeared. But most of all I just remember crying, desolated that I had had to leave. Would I ever come back? I didn't know.

A Gift Given

It was that night in Dubrovnik, when the precious Lady reached out to me again. I could almost hear her. "My dear daughter, you have come at my call though you didn't know it then. And you have listened to me and responded. You have stood on my hill and I have blessed you. You have been given a great gift in coming here. How many others long to come and cannot? Can you not be a little grateful for what you have been given?"

I knelt by my bed that night, something I haven't done since I was a little girl, and I prayed with a joyful and happy heart then. Yes, I had been given a wonderful gift, a gift that didn't end just because I had to leave. The wonder of God and the tender love of his Mother had been shown to me in a special way. I was loved. I was blessed. And I knew that Medjugorje would always be with me in the innermost part of my being.

* * * * * *

The Flight Home

Normally pilgrims leave Medjugorje in the morning and are taken to Dubrovnik overnight. The next day can be a tiring and debilitating one as it usually involves a long flight home and, quite often, a layover in some European city for a few hours. As I (Father Ruane) see it, there are some advantages to this seemingly "wasted" day. It gives us pilgrims time to reflect on our experience and share our thoughts and prayers with the rest of the group.

Arrival at an airport in the U.S. signals the return to the reality of daily life and routine. Jet lag is a factor at first, but it does go away. The memories of Medjugorje and its spirit of prayer, penance, and radical concentration on the things of God and his Mother usually remain.

But the return to home and everyday life brings with it a challenge, integrating the Medjugorje experience into that everydayness. Some people seem to accomplish that easily. Others find it more difficult. Some, unfortunately and almost immediately, get sucked back into their former routines, and some even lapse back into sinful ways and patterns of being.

One person fell back so quickly into his old way of life that he decided that he had to get back to Medjugorje as soon as possible. He did go back and it helped. He was able to return home with greater determination to live the messages of our Lady.

Speaking with different people and their experiences of "returning home" put one very much in mind of Jesus' parable about the seed that falls on good earth or rocky ground (Matthew 13). All of us may at times seem to be like the "rocky soil" type and we may experience the same or similar difficulties as the man mentioned in the last paragraph. The good news is that even rocky ground in the tender care of our Lord and his Mother can be made into good earth.

There are even some people who return home, pack their bags, and go to live in Medjugorje. But very **few** of us can do that, and we are **sure** that only a very few are called by God to do that. Most often God is calling us to live the message of the Gospel (which is what the Medjugorje messages are) right where we live and work.

* * * * * *

OUR PRAYER FOR YOU

We hope in this book to share some insights, our own and others', on living out in our daily lives the message of Medjugorje, to answer our Lady's call right where we live and work. The reason she has come to Medjugorje is to reiterate what God wants from us and to invite us to respond to his invitation to holiness.

Whether or not you have been to Medjugorje, the "Medjugorje experience" can be yours. If you open your heart to the workings of the Spirit, read and pray over our Lady's messages, and then apply them to the ways in which you live, you can be part of the enormous network of people around the world who are trying to make a difference.

It is our prayer as you read this book that you will feel deeply in your life the presence of Jesus and his Mother and that as you grow in your commitment to living the message, you will hear her say to you, "Thank you for hearing my call."

CHAPTER 3

Two Pilgrims' Progress

FATHER RUANE'S STORY

Once Was Not Enough

Once was not enough for me. As you already know, I have gone to Medjugorje four times within eight months. The first time I had a great experience and yet was still a little cautious about everything. The second time I went with a deep longing for quiet with the Lord and his Mother. I call that my retreat pilgrimage as God granted me my heart's desire for a time of quiet prayer with just the right mix of socializing with a beautiful group of people.

The third time, my Holy Week pilgrimage, I went with mixed feelings because of some personal differences with the leader of the group. We had attempted to talk it out before the pilgrimage, but we were really not meant for each other. That was a drawback and there were some major difficulties with lodgings that disrupted the group's unity. However, even that pilgrimage had great blessings of peace and prayer as we all grappled with the problems and, in a few days, felt the special blessings of Medjugorje: peace and a sense of perspective which allowed forgiveness to be given and received and for the healing process to begin. Those pilgrims are some of my best and dearest Medjugorje friends.

The fourth time was my Pentecost and Priesthood pilgrimage and was a great blessing for those reasons and because of the basic unity and love of the people who traveled with me.

However, as I said at the beginning of this chapter, once was not enough. I needed all four trips to Medjugorje. The second time reinforced what I had heard the first time. The third time made me realize that Medjugorje is an earthly paradise that can have difficulties . . . with pilgrims, with the stresses and strains of travel, with hardships . . . but that all these difficulties are a call to prayer and to embracing the cross. The fourth experience was a mountaintop experience even when we were in the valley at Saint James Church because spiritual mountaintops come in the most amazing places.

Sharing the Blessings

Some people may not be able to go even once. Others may go only once. I know I have been blessed in being able to go so often. I know God wants me to share those blessings with people. And my hope here is that what I share will in some way help you to experience Medjugorje if you have not been there or to help deepen your commitment if you have. I pray that what will be written here will be a blessing for many. It is a blessing for me even to write it because it forces me to reflect and pray and expend some effort in getting all my thoughts in order. Mainly, it helps me get into perspective what our Lord and our Lady wanted me to receive and now to share about Medjugorje.

One young man I met in Medjugorje had a rather successful career in the stock market and had gone to Medjugorje, heard the message, and returned home just long enough to give everything he had to the poor, then went back to Medjugorje. After a few months there, he went on to Fatima and worked around the grounds of the basilica in order to pay for his room and board. He spent a great deal of time there in prayer and reflection on the Fatima message, reading again the accounts of the various apparitions and the writings of Sister Lucia and others about Fatima. His conclusion was that our Lord has used our Lady at the beginning and the end of the twentieth century to give his message, a message that is the same in both places.

Now it seems to me that in Medjugorje the urgency is even greater. The appearances are more frequent and even more intense. I believe that is because the situation of the world requires it. It is time to move. Our Lord is being very patient. He keeps sending the same message to us through his Mother. But now at Medjugorje he is being most insistent. **Pray. Fast. Repent. Convert. The time is now.**

Apparition Hill

During my first pilgrimage I had decided to keep my focus on the church. In fact, on the first full day in Medjugorje, I had gotten up early and gone to the 7:30 Croatian Mass, had breakfast, and then went back to church for the English Mass at 10:00 a.m. Then I took a walk, had lunch and a well-deserved rest. By then it was time for the rosary at 5:00 p.m. in the church, followed by another Croatian Mass to which all the pilgrims are invited.

On the second afternoon around 3:00, four of our pilgrims were going to Apparition Hill where our Lady first appeared. They asked me to accompany them. As we began to walk, we took out our rosaries and began to pray. It's amazing how automatic that becomes in Medjugorje. Whenever you are going to or from some place, your hand automatically goes for your rosary and the other people do the same. They are only too happy to join in that beautiful prayer. Sometimes on the hill or mountain or in the church, one group will be praying the rosary in their own language and others just join right in and respond in their own languages. Surprisingly, everyone's words seem to fit in with the others to form a beautiful chorus of praise to God and honor to his Blessed Mother.

Our Lord's words about two or three being gathered in his name take on a special meaning in Medjugorje!

And so we prayed the rosary as we climbed the hill. Then we separated and became quiet. At the spot of the first apparition there is a cross with a mound of stones at its base on which many candles have been placed. It was a sunny day but quite windy and many of the flames had gone out. I started to relight some of the candles when all of a sudden I stopped as the significance of what I had been doing struck me and I prayed a very fervent prayer.

"Lord Jesus Christ, through the intercession of your Lady Mother, I ask you to relight the fires of my priestly zeal. Renew the fervor of my priesthood. Relight my fire."

I had just finished twenty-two months as pastor of a rather large and well-to-do parish in our Archdiocese. Most of my time as pastor had been spent restoring and redecorating the parish plant: the church and school; working on the spiritual and organizational renewal of the parish; plus handling some rather difficult staff problems. This was a stressful period and had a physical effect on me. I developed an alarmingly low heart rate which, coupled with my enlarged heart and its murmur, made things seem quite serious. My internist of twenty-nine years had died just at that time, and so I was left in competent but unfamiliar hands which did not help the situation.

All of this convinced the Archbishop that it was probably wise for me to take a sabbatical to do some resting, writing, and traveling. Even before I agreed to this and resigned my pastorate effective three months later, things had improved immensely. New personnel came on the staff and the repairs were accomplished more quickly than we had anticipated. Though the first sixteen months of my pastorate had seemed like a sharing in the Lord's crucifixion, the last six months were an exhilarating experience of his resurrection!

Father Ruane celebrates Mass in the Apparition Room at St. James Church.

I did enjoy those last few months a great deal and certainly celebrated the good we had been able to do together. I left with great satisfaction for a job well done, but also with a sense of incompleteness. My dream had been to be part of that parish community for the next ten or twelve years. But that was not to be.

On Apparition Hill that day, I knew the flame of my priestly zeal was still burning, but I felt quite drained from the pastoral experience and realized a need to get reenergized. Our Lady seemed to have a significant part to play in that effort and where better to begin than on this hill?

There was a certain sense of melancholy, if not actual depression, coloring my mood at that time. In my head I knew I had done the right thing, and in my heart I knew it was right. But somewhere in my gut I was feeling a vague discontent. We spiritual directors often say, "God speaks to us in our gut," which means we need to respect what God is saying through our gut and listen to that, as well as to our heads and our hearts.

As I prayed on Apparition Hill that first day, all of this was somewhere within me, perhaps buried under quite a blanket of rationalizations. (I'm good at that.) Thank God it surfaced. And thanks be to God I was able to place the whole situation before him and his Blessed Mother.

I did not feel an immediate response to my prayer, but I did receive a jump start of my priestly battery, a definite recharging. This became evident to me a bit later when I went to Rome and was able to say Mass at St. Peter's several times. This completed the process by reconnecting me to my roots as a Roman Catholic, as a priest, and as an amateur Church historian.

Originally I had gone to Medjugorje to see a renewed parish, and I did. But the experience had a deeper impact on me as priest and as person. I went there at the call of our Lord and his Lady Mother to experience a relighting of my fire and zeal as his man, follower, and priest.

I returned to Apparition Hill one other time during my first pilgrimage, and again was blessed by a special time of peaceful prayer.

But another memorable time on Apparition Hill was on the first Friday of February during my second visit, my retreat week at Medjugorje. It was cold and quite dark, almost 10:30 in the evening. We were there for an apparition of our Lady to Ivan, the leader of a prayer group for young people.

A sudden silence descended as she appeared to Ivan. In that silence one of the members of our group touched my arm and said, "Look there, Father. Look at the cross." I stared out into the night and there on Mt. Krizevac the cross (thirty-five feet tall and fourteen tons of concrete) was illumined. It seemed as if a huge torch had been placed on the vertical bar just as it crosses the horizontal bar. In the message that night our Lady said she would leave a sign on the cross and in the light.

As we walked down the hill, we people (perhaps two hundred of us) were visibly excited, having prayed together and having listened to the translation of our Lady's message that night. She said that she was blessing all of us who were there and all those whom we carried in our hearts.

Every once in a while, as we went home that night, I checked to make sure that the cross was still lighted. When I got to the house where I was staying, I lingered outside on the road, looking at the cross and thinking what a beautiful sign it was.

A few minutes after I had gone inside, a couple from our group joined me. I mentioned the lighted cross. They hadn't seen it. We went outside again, but the light had gone out on the cross at Krizevac. I quietly prayed that my light would not go out but would shine even more brightly. Pray with me that it will.

Mount Krizevac

The first time I climbed Krizevac I did so as the leader of a group of about forty-three people. We made the ascent at a gentle pace because some of our group were elderly. We prayed at each of the stations of the cross, using Father Slavko's prayer book, **Pray With the Heart.** I was trying to get as many people involved as possible, saying the prayers or doing the readings, and also to keep them together. I felt distracted by the responsibility of caring for so many people.

At one point there was a commotion at the edge of our group as the links of someone's rosary turned gold. For that particular person, it was a very special moment. But nonetheless, it was a distraction from our prayers. I had wanted to have the pilgrims pray with special fervor on our journey to each of the stations and especially when we arrived at the top of the mountain where the huge cross is situated. But it was hard keeping them together and focused on the Way of the Cross.

I felt weighed down by having to care for these people. One part of me wanted to be free, to go at my own pace and to pray my own prayers. Another part of me was saying, "This is what it means to be a shepherd and that's what you claim to be. You have a responsibility for these people, so why not center your thoughts on the cross of Jesus and do your best?" And that's just what I did.

In some ways that experience reminded me of making the stations of the cross in Jerusalem in 1964. As a symbolic gesture, we took turns carrying a wooden cross through the streets. We walked along the Via Dolorosa, stopping to pray very fervently at each station. However, we were terribly distracted by all the hustle and bustle of the store owners' hawking their wares at the top of their lungs. They had gotten so used to pilgrims walking through their streets carrying a cross that they never even looked in our direction. And they certainly didn't lower the volume of their bargaining.

It was distracting. It wasn't pious. It wasn't fervent. But that is almost certainly just the way it was when Jesus carried his cross.

That memory of making the stations in Jerusalem was a reminder to me that I have chosen to subordinate my desires to those of the Lord. At times I may not have the luxury of being quiet and pious and fervent as I may want. That is very likely part of my cross. Each of us has to carry our own cross up some pretty rough hills, but never alone, as we carry it in union with Jesus.

My cross at times may not be an inanimate object, but the people whom the Lord has given me to love and serve. I don't say that people are my cross lightly or with any sense of superiority since I am quite well aware of the fact that some people may regard me as part of their cross.

My prayer on Mt. Krizevac was really just a quick offering of everything that was going on in union with Christ crucified. My prayer now is a little bit more developed, but the essence is the same: "Jesus, teach me to carry the cross that you have fashioned for me. Help me, Lord, for without your help I fall and I fail to be the shepherd after your own heart that both you and I want me to be. Help me, Jesus, to recognize that the cross you give me will lead me to eternal life. And I thank you, Jesus, for the crosses you have sent into my life."

Krizevac — the Mountain of the Cross — and a priest named Ruane were meant for each other for the Ruane family motto is: "Cresco per crucem," "I grow through the cross." And the only way that I am going to be able to grow is by accepting my cross and if I carry it with Jesus who alone makes it possible to do so. Mt. Krizevac has a great appeal for me. When I was in Medjugorje in February on my retreat I didn't climb it, but it still dominated much of my thoughts and I gazed at it from many different vantage points.

In April I climbed it on Good Friday with my sister Elenore and her roommate Rosalie. Actually I was feeling miserable. I had a sore throat, nasal congestion, and a great bronchial cough by then. However, I had said I would go with them and I really did want to make sure they made it to the top. We all made it and our prayers were especially blessed by the intimate connection we felt with the Lord as we three climbed with him to the top of cross mountain on that special Friday. The wind at the top was fierce, so we only stayed a few minutes, but it was well worth the effort.

On my last day in Medjugorje in June, I climbed the mountain by myself, but for my sister Marie's intentions. She and her daughter (who had turned her ankle) had not climbed Krizevac and we were leaving that day. I enjoyed the solitary climb and the prayers, the beauty of the day, and the loveliness of the view of the valley and the Church of Saint James.

* * * * * *

SISTER RUTHANN'S STORY

Lord, Help My Unbelief

In November 1989 I flew to Medjugorje, confident, strong, and deeply committed to my unbelief in what was supposedly happening there. On the plane, while others prayed the rosary or read books on the apparitions, I read a novel, watched the movie, slept.

So why did I go? Because I had been asked to go as a spiritual director for a group of pilgrims and, what the heck? It was a free trip to Yugoslavia. My disbelief did not seem to me to be an insuperable obstacle to my ministry as spiritual director. After all, a director is not there to impose his or her views on the directee, but to listen, to pray, and to be open to whatever the Spirit is doing in the one being directed. God being God, of course, sometimes the director, too, is "surprised by the Spirit." But that possibility was far from my mind as we zoomed over the Atlantic.

The first four days I was there I was happy to attend Mass, especially the Croatian Mass because the singing was so beautiful, slightly less happy to keep praying the rosary, delighted to stroll through the fields and enjoy the peace which spoke so strongly to me of the presence of God. Those few days were a little retreat for me, despite having to listen to "fantastic tales" of rosaries turning gold; and I thoroughly enjoyed my time there. I stayed away from Apparition Hill, Mt. Krizevac, Father Jozo, and (with the exception of Ivan) the visionaries. That was a part of the scene that I could do without, thank you very much.

In those days I became steadily more convinced that we see, hear, experience what we want to see, hear, experience, as people told of seeing the sun dance. Me? I was just happy the sun was out!

Mt. Krizevac

On Friday we climbed Mt. Krizevac; so, of course, I went along. We stopped as we climbed to pray the Stations of the Cross, a devotion which I usually love. But there were so many of us that the prayer seemed to lose its meaning for me and I heartily wished that I could be alone, either on this rocky path or in my room or in church. Somewhere. Just alone. For if there is one "sacrifice" that must be made on a pilgrimage to Medjugorje, it is — for me, at least — the absolute lack of "alone time." The church is always crowded. The hills-cum-mountains are always pulsing with pilgrims. And there is a roommate, in my case a friend with a nine-month-old baby. Never mind that both friend and baby were wonderful. They were. But I crave, need healthy doses of solitude. I was not to have them.

When we finally got to the top of Krizevac I was grateful to be able to catch my breath and rest a little. Ignorant as I was of nearly all things Medjugorjean, I didn't know the story of the cross on the mountain (the villagers erected it in 1933 to celebrate the 1900th anniversary of the death and resurrection of our Lord), nor did I particularly care. Nor did I know that our Lady is reported to have said that she goes there frequently at dawn to pray. It was just a mountain with a cross on the top and a really spectacular view of the village on one side and the mountain range on the other. So as soon as I could gracefully make my exit, I did, descending the path rather more hastily than I had ascended it.

Alone at last!

That evening a small number of our group of pilgrims asked me if I would climb (groan!) Apparition Hill the next day to pray the rosary with them. How could I say no? So I agreed, masking my reluctance with a smile.

A Short Detour

Now I have to make a small detour here to fill in the background for what was about to happen. My mother and I have had a rather difficult relationship, somewhat complicated by her emotional illness and my own proclivity (from infancy) for independence. I have, depending on circumstances, been either daughter or mother to her. The reverse has held true as well. I have loved her and not loved her. She has loved me and not loved me. You get the general picture, I'm sure.

Apparition Hill

The last few years have been among the harder times and, after a visit home in June of 1986, I decided that it would perhaps be best for both of us if I stayed away for a while. I continued to pray for her healing and the healing of our relationship, but the situation was just too stressful for me to handle. And that's how matters remained until the afternoon of November 11, 1989, when I stood on the Hill of Apparition.

The evening before, one of the men on the trip had given me a rosary, crystal beads and — in the place where there is normally a miraculous medal — a small container holding a tiny rock and some soil from Medjugorje. He knew that I would be climbing Apparition Hill the next day and he asked me to take that particular rosary with me. Why not? So I did, climbing with the small group to recite the rosary when we reached the top.

The site of the apparitions attained, I began to lead the first decade of the joyful mysteries, the Annunciation. Suddenly I was overwhelmed with light, a light that I cannot describe. It was all light gathered and there was no small place of shadow. First the light, then warmth, then an overwhelming sense of love. Somehow the hill was no longer there and I just was . . . in some place of light. And I heard Mary speak to me.

She spoke to me about my mother and her healing for which I had so long prayed. And about Mary's own mothering of me, and oh, so many things. I felt myself healed of an old and great pain. Then she said, "There is something you must do for me today." And the light went away and I was back on the hill still leading the rosary, watching the sunlight dance through the crystal beads, and feeling more at peace than I ever had before in my life.

Of course, my terribly rational self then had to deny that the whole thing had happened at all. Which I tried to do. I decided that I was "suffering" from religious hysteria and the best course of action would be to forget the whole thing. So I practically raced down the hill when the rosary was finished, determined to get back to my cozy, comfortable, and non-believing self.

Later that afternoon Father Ruane led a healing service in the rotunda behind the church. It was a beautiful experience and powerful. The Spirit was moving in a myriad of ways and it was good to be there. After the service I stayed to pray with Father and a small group over a young man who had asked for special prayers. We prayed with him a long time and again the feeling of peace and powerful healing was present. When he had gone, Father headed for the church and the evening rosary and Mass. But the sun had gone down and I was cold, so I decided to go back to the house instead.

Father went into the church and I continued to walk alongside it when all at once I heard her again. "That is what you had to do for me," she said. I stopped in my tracks and looked up. The tower of Saint James was glowing with a light that was neither electric nor candle. I wish I could explain it but, honestly, it is a light that I cannot compare to any other thing in my earthly experience. It was the light I remembered from the afternoon, a light in which there is no shadow or shading. It is just pure light. I saw. I heard. And I could deny her presence no longer.

That evening after dinner, despite my firm intellectual resolve to keep the whole thing to myself lest everyone else think I was crazy, I shared my experience with the group. I didn't intend to, not even as I got to my feet and felt the tears begin. But someone stronger than I took over. The wonderful thing was that no one thought I was hallucinating. They listened with respect and love, an attitude typical of pilgrims, I've discovered.

Confirmation?

The next morning one of the men came up to me and asked, "Sister, do you need confirmation of what happened yesterday?" "Not really," I replied smiling. "I **know** it happened."

"All the same," he said, "I'd like to tell you. At the time you said you saw the light in the tower last night, Ivan was in the tower and the Blessed Mother was appearing to him."

I went back to the hill that afternoon . . . just to say thank you, oblivious now to the souvenir shops and the candle vendors along the path. None of that mattered anymore because I knew our Lady was there, touching and blessing in the name of her Son even the most hardened of hearts. She was there and so was I. What greater gift could I ask?

Only the Beginning

That was my last day in Medjugorje. Or perhaps it was my first. Because that was really the beginning of my conversion, of my hearing her messages, or my first feeble attempts to incorporate what I could into my life. Needless to say, I clung to that crystal rosary for the rest of the trip, knowing that somehow my relationship with my mother was going to be healed.

I prayed with that rosary as I walked the wall around Old Dubrovnik and as I knelt in awe at St. Peter's in Rome. It was in my hand as the Holy Father gave us his blessing from his window high above St. Peter's Square and it was still in my hand as I rode the bus back from the Vatican to the house of a friend where I was staying.

As the plane soared back across the Atlantic to New York, Father Ruane said something to me about the rosary being so special and how I would use it for the rest of my life. Without even stopping to think about it, I said, "No, I have to send it to my mother."

I did send it to her, wrapped as a Christmas present with a note that on Christmas day I would call her and tell her all about it. But I didn't. Instead I went home and told her in person. I took my mother not just the story of a rosary and a windy hilltop, but a daughter healed at last to be free to love her as Mary had whispered to me.

And, of course, everyone wants to know, is my mother well? That depends on how you define "well." Her illness continues, on again, off again, though generally she seems to be better than she has been in a while. And she overcame her dread of flying to come to New Jersey in June to be present as I made my final vows. She even says she's coming back next year. And that's what I thought Mary was talking about that day. But I realize now that the healing she promised was a healing of a different sort. It was the healing of my heart which helped me to realize that all that had been wounded in our mother and daughter relationship could not be laid at my mother's door, that indeed I was not only wounded, I had done some of the wounding, that I too stood in need of forgiveness.

Is my mother "well"? Am I "well"? Are we "well" together? Yes. And that is a much greater healing than what I had imagined or hoped for. Such is the Mother of God.

Home Is Not the End

But my pilgrimage to Medjugorje is far from over. In the last ten months I have read the books, listened to the cassettes, watched the videos. More than anything else, I have prayed and prayed and prayed. And I have attempted and am still attempting to incorporate the messages into my life.

As we go through this book I will continue to share those bits and pieces and mighty moments with you. But twice since my return our Lady has taken a strong hand in keeping me turned toward Apparition Hill. And I'd like to tell you those stories right now.

On February 15 I began a thirty-day retreat. And since I'm being honest, I have to admit that I had been a little casual about saying all fifteen decades of the rosary each day. Most, well, many days I managed it; but some days I sort of slid by with one set of mysteries. That evening as I prowled around the retreat house to get my bearings, I went into the tape room. The room is filled with shelves and drawers which, in turn, are filled with audio cassettes. I walked into the room and over to a set of shelves, quite at random. And literally, the first tape my eyes went to (and it was just jumbled in among all the others) was called "Kraljici Mira" which means "Queen of Peace" in Croatian. I picked it up, smiled, said to her, "Okay, so you want to go on retreat with me?" and took the tape back to my room. It is a recording of the people of Medjugorje singing their hymns to our Lord and his Lady Mother. I began each day of my retreat listening to them and seeing in my mind's eye that glowing tower on an autumn night in Yugoslavia.

The tape moved me, challenged me to take the messages even more seriously. Well, I didn't have any Medjugorje books with me, such reading material being discouraged on a thirty-day Ignatian retreat. But one message I could remember without any help was her call to pray, pray the rosary — all fifteen decades every day. And so I did (and do).

Gifts Given

Well, it seems that Mary is just about as generous as her Son when it comes to giving gifts (maybe he inherited it from her as well as from his Father). Because as I sat or knelt or walked each day meditating on those fifteen mysteries, poems arose from my heart which I believe are among the best I've ever written. I'll have more to say on that when we get to a discussion of the rosary, but I had to mention it here as that retreat really gave me the time and space and quiet to let my own Medjugorje experience take root.

The second experience is not so dramatic. There are even those who would just laugh and shrug it off. But it was wonderful for me . . . and I'm one of those people who cannot believe in "coincidence."

Mir, Mir

A few months ago the sisters with whom I live and I decided that we would go to Washington, D.C., for a weekend of being together, something we rarely have time to do because of the diversity of our ministries and schedules. Well, it seemed a wonderful idea at the time, but as the weekend drew closer I was really dreading it. I was very tired. The Summit Conference between Bush and Gorbachev would be going on and heaven only knew how that might tie the city up in knots. Because of one of our schedules we couldn't leave **for** Washington until after 5:00 p.m. on Friday and because of another one's schedule, we were going to have to leave **from** Washington shortly after dawn on Sunday. The whole trip seemed less and less attractive the closer it got and I tried to persuade the others to cancel it. I was not successful in that attempt.

I was feeling really rotten about the whole thing, angry and tired and disgusted. But you take the bitter with the sweet in community life, so there was no question of my not going. So I prayed. I prayed for peace with the decision we as a community had made and with the weekend. I just asked the Lord for peace of heart (and nice weather if he could manage it).

On Tuesday night when I went to bed I reiterated my prayer. Just make me peaceful about it, Lord, please. Wednesday morning as I awoke but before my eyes were even opened, I heard a bird in the tree outside my bedroom window. He was chirping into the rising sun for all he was worth: "Mir. Mir. Mir. Mir." ("Mir" is the Croatian word for peace.)

And I laughed right out loud. I asked for peace and I got it, in the birdsong and — more important — in my heart, I realized. The Prince of Peace had answered my prayer and the Queen of Peace had set it to music for me.

My Medjugorje saga continues.

THE MESSAGE OF MEDJUGORJE

Our Lady Proposes a Five-Point Plan

*** Commitment to God ***
Let God rule your life.
Begin by turning
from sin.

*** Faith ***
It is your lifeline
to God, so live
by it.

*** Prayer ***
Regular Mass,
monthly confession,
complete rosary daily
— these top the list.

*** Fasting ***
Bread and water on
Wednesday and Friday,
if possible.

*** Peace ***
In yourself, in your
relationships,
in our world.

CHAPTER 4

Reflecting on Commitment

In this day and age the word commitment is not much honored. Instead it is joked about, shrugged off, smiled at, and often used as an excuse to end a relationship prematurely, as in "I'm just not ready to make a commitment." Happily it can also give rise to the truth, to lifelong pledges made and kept, to vows proclaimed and lived. What **does** commitment mean and what does it have to do with Medjugorje?

A Matter of Mind and Heart

I (Sister Ruthann) think that almost more than anything else a commitment is a mind set. I know there are those who would take exception to that and say that a commitment is a matter of the heart, of feeling. And that's partially true. But commitment, faithfulness to a promise, dedication to a certain behavior is, very often, a matter of will. I have promised "such and such" and so I will live it, no matter how I am feeling. Even if my promise or attempt is made just "one day at a time."

Commitment cannot depend on feeling. In a rush of religious fervor, in the trembling of first love, in the passion of almost any moment, we can make promises. But time passes. Fervor, trembling, passion fade and we are left with the reality of a commitment.

Fortunately for me, my "commitment" to living the message of Medjugorje did not come in an instant. It is a living and growing thing: a small shoot here, a tiny blossom there, giving promise of what is yet to come. So I guess I would have to say that my commitment at this moment is to the root. I know what I am called to do. I pray for the grace to do it and, when I fail, I simply go back to the root for nourishment and try, try again.

* * * * * *

A Personal Echo

For me (Father Ruane) commitment to the Gospel-based messages of Medjugorje is my personal echo of the Son's "yes" uttered to the Father's plan before the Incarnation and the "yes" of Jesus at Gethsemane to God's will. Jesus tore that "yes" from his lips almost frozen with fear in anticipation of his bitter sufferings, passion, and death. He lived his "yes" always.

My commitment is an echo of Mary's own "yes" to the angel Gabriel's invitation to her to be the Mother of God's Son — Jesus, the Messiah.

As I have mentioned, I did not come to a full-bodied commitment until after my third pilgrimage. Until then, human respect and wanting to be thought of as a sophisticated erudite priest-theologian held me back. But one day I had to face the contradiction between my words (cool and slightly detached) and my actions (geared to promoting the messages). That was a time of grace for me. Thank God for his patience.

I hear in our Lady's messages at Medjugorje recurring themes from her appearances in Guadalupe in Mexico in 1531, the Rue de Bac and the Miraculous Medal, in France at Lourdes in 1858, and in Fatima in 1917.

* * * * * *

Why a Commitment?

Why make a commitment to the message of Medjugorje? Because to me (Sister Ruthann) it makes sense. Our Lady's call is the Gospel call. Her urging, the urging of her Son. The goal, salvation for all. But why would I, born and raised a Catholic, now living a vowed life in a religious community, feel the need to make a commitment beyond that? Because, my brothers and sisters in Christ, I — as many of you — find it easy to be a tepid Christian. I — as many of you — can stretch out, oh so comfortably onto the chaise lounge of our culture. I — as many of you — can settle for mediocrity. I can, in fact, be a "good Catholic" and a perfectly (well, imperfectly) satisfactory Caldwell Dominican without fasting twice a week or praying fifteen decades of the rosary every day. So why?

Our Lady's challenge at Medjugorje calls us to get back to Gospel values and to remember who it is who saves us. There is an urgency about her appearances and messages that bids us to remember that indeed we know neither the hour nor the day. Whenever we read one of her messages and take it to prayer, like the percussion section of an orchestra we may hear beneath her melody the words from the Ash Wednesday reading: "**Now** is the acceptable hour. **Now** is the day of salvation."

* * * * * *

The Heart of Her Message

So that is our "why." The "how" is meat for the rest of this book. But as we read through the thousands of messages she has given us, perhaps we might pause. Are some of her requests (and they are requests, never commands) more important than others? We think so.

She says, "Pray, pray, pray." She says, "Fast." She says, "Read Scripture." She says, "Go to confession." She says, "Make Mass the center of your lives."

It seems that these five requests, repeated hundreds of times over the past nine years, are the heart of her message. They are her plan, in the name of her Son, for peace and the salvation of the world. It is these five heavenly invitations which will form the main body of this book, our experiences and reflections on these invitations, and some ways we have found to live them out in our own lives. It is our prayer that as the Virgin speaks to your heart perhaps some of our words will help you to live what she asks, to make a commitment to conversion.

"Pray in order that you may be able to comprehend all that I am giving here. You know that without prayer you cannot understand all that God is planning through each one of you. Therefore, pray! . . . I invite you. I need you. I chose you. You are important. . . . Without you I am not able to help the world."

CHAPTER 5

Return to the Gospel

"Dear children, I beseech you, listen to my messages and live them, so I can guide you" (January 8, 1987).

Lacking official "approval" of the Church, the messages of our Lady hang suspended between heaven and earth. Some accept them wholeheartedly, while others are waiting for the Vatican to make a statement. Some are afraid to listen in case there might be false doctrine. Some, of course, just refuse to hear anything that might upset their comfortable lives. For these last, there is little we can do but pray. For the others, we believe, there is comfort in knowing that our Lady's messages are her Son's messages and those messages have not changed in 2000 years. Medjugorje is not a new revelation. It is a reminder of what has been ever since Jesus walked the earth.

* * * * * *

An Emphatic Yes

When I (Father Ruane) first heard the messages and especially our Lady's five-point plan for responding to her call, I felt rising deep within me an emphatic "Yes, this is Jesus' way!" I've never had to change my mind nor disown that original gut-level affirmation. It has only grown stronger as I have read and studied, prayed and reflected on the messages.

When I returned from my fourth pilgrimage (the Pentecost/Priesthood one), I brought back a thousand holy cards which were distributed in our newsletter and at our services. On one side was a beautiful picture of our Lady with the words, "Queen of Peace, pray for us!" On the other side was an explanation of the call from Mary, her plan for peace. She proposes a program in five interrelated parts.

The Five-Point Plan

1. **Commitment to God.** Let him rule your life. Begin by turning away from sin.

2. **Faith.** It's your lifeline to God. Therefore, live by it.

3. **Prayer.** Regular Mass, monthly confession, the complete rosary and other prayers each day including prayerful reading of the Scriptures.

4. **Fasting.** Bread and water each Wednesday and Friday if you can. If not, at least cut back on your intake of food and refrain from various other activities.

5. **Peace.** In yourself, in your human relations, in our war-threatened world. Peace is God's gift in response to the other four parts of the plan.

Come, Follow Me!

I hope that God speaks to your deep inner being as you read this plan for peace and gives you a conviction that what we have here is the call of Christ to "Come! Follow me!"

The mystical side of me (which I conceal rather well) knew that right away and the analytical part of my personality has yielded (quite uncharacteristically) to that conviction. Sister Ruthann, on the other hand, has done a splendid job of comparing the words of our Lord in the Gospel with those of our Lady at Medjugorje.

St. James Church from across the field.

Please read what follows ever so carefully. May you come to an acceptance of the messages in her way or my way or whatever way God uses for you.

* * * * * *

The Gospel and Medjugorje

One of the reasons I (Sister Ruthann) have found it so easy to believe the messages of Medjugorje (if not always finding it so easy to put them into practice) is because Mary's words are Gospel-based. She is not promulgating some unfamiliar truth. She is not revealing anything we have not known for hundreds and hundreds of years. She is, most blessedly and not surprisingly, only reiterating what her Son said and said and said again.

The poet in me is always tempted to find elegant ways of speaking, to intertwine and interject words in ways that will soothe or startle or seduce. But for this portion, I will resist all such temptations. I shall simply quote Mary and Jesus, point and counterpoint, to illustrate how her words today echo what Jesus said so long ago.

Prayer

Mary tells us to pray: "Dear children, again I call you to prayer with the heart" (1/23/86). "I call you to approach prayer actively. You wish to live everything I am telling you, but you are not succeeding because you are not praying. Dear children, I beseech you to open yourselves and begin to pray. Prayer will be your joy" (3/20/86).

And Jesus says: "Pray for those who persecute you" (Matthew 5:44). "This is how you are to pray: Our Father in heaven, hallowed be your name . . ." (Matthew 6:12-14). "Ask and it will be given to you; seek and you will find; knock and the door will be opened to you" (Matthew 7:7 and Luke

11:9). "Again I say to you, if two of you agree on earth about anything for which they are to pray, it shall be granted to them by my heavenly Father. For where two or three are gathered in my name, there am I in the midst of them" (Matthew 18:19-20). "Whatever you ask for in prayer with faith, you will receive" (Matthew 21:22). "Watch and pray that you may not undergo the test" (Matthew 26:41). "Therefore I tell you, all that you ask for in prayer, believe that you will receive it and it shall be yours" (Mark 11:24). "Be vigilant at all times and pray that you have the strength to escape the tribulations that are imminent and to stand before the Son of Man" (Luke 21:36). "If you remain in me and my words remain in you, ask for whatever you want and it will be done for you" (John 15:7). "Until now you have not asked anything in my name; ask and you will receive, so that your joy may be complete" (John 16:24).

Fasting

Mary wishes us to fast: "The best fast is on bread and water" (7/21/82). "The devil tries to impose his power on you, but you must remain strong and persevere in your faith. You have to pray and fast" (11/81).

Jesus, who himself fasted, did not give strict instructions to fast. Rather, he seems to have taken for granted that his followers would fast and so spoke from that perspective. "When you fast, do not look gloomy like the hypocrites. . . . But when you fast, anoint your head and wash your face so that you may not appear to be fasting, except to your Father who is hidden" (Matthew 6:16-18). "Can the wedding guests fast while the bridegroom is with them? As long as they have the bridegroom with them they cannot fast. But the days will come when the bridegroom is taken away from them, and then they will fast" (Mark 2:19-20 and Luke 5:33-35).

Scripture

Our Lady invites us to read the Scriptures. "Dear children, today I call you to read the Bible every day in your homes and let it be in a visible place so as always to encourage you to read it and to pray" (10/18/84).

Jesus quoted Scripture over and over again during his ministry. He acknowledged that "they testify on my behalf" (John 5:39). And in at least two places we are told that "Jesus then opened their minds to understand the scriptures" (Luke 24:45 and Luke 24:27 and 32).

Confession

Mary begs us, "Pray, pray! It is necessary to believe firmly, to go to confession regularly, and, likewise, to receive Holy Communion. It is the only salvation" (2/10/82).

It is an echo of the call of her Son: "Repent, for the kingdom of heaven is at hand" (Matthew 4:17). "Do you think because these Galileans suffered in this way they were greater sinners than all other Galileans? By no means! But I tell you, if you do not repent, you will all perish as they did!" (Luke 13:2-3). "Thus it is written that the Messiah would suffer and rise from the dead on the third day and that repentance, for the forgiveness of sins, would be preached in his name to all nations" (Luke 24:46-47). And beautifully, "Receive the holy Spirit. Whose sins you forgive are forgiven them, and whose sins you retain are retained" (John 20:22-23).

Eucharist

Our holy Mother says, "There are many of you who have sensed the beauty of the Holy Mass. Jesus gives you his graces in the Mass" (4/3/86). "Let the Holy Mass be your life" (4/25/88).

In reverence and joy we recall the words of Jesus: "Take and eat; this is my body. . . . Drink from this cup, all of you, for this is my blood of the covenant, which will be shed on behalf of many for the forgiveness of sins" (Matthew 26:26-28). "Do this in memory of me" (Luke 22:19).

Conversion/Evangelization

"I have come to call the world to conversion for the last time," says Mary (5/2/82). "My Son suffers very much because the world is not converting. May the world be converted and make peace" (9/26/83). "I am calling you to the light which you should carry to all the people who are in darkness. . . . Dear children, give them the light" (3/14/85).

And Jesus says, "You are the light of the world. A city set on a mountain cannot be hidden. Nor do they light a lamp and then put it under a bushel basket; it is set on a lampstand, where it gives light to all in the house. Just so, your light must shine before others that they may see your good deeds and glorify your heavenly Father" (Matthew 5:14-16). And in his last thundering words, recorded by Matthew: "Go, therefore, and make disciples of all nations, baptizing them in the name of the Father, and of the Son, and of the holy Spirit, teaching them to observe all that I have commanded you" (Matthew 28:19-20).

The Call to Gospel Holiness

We need not hesitate to answer our Lady's call, for it is the call of her Son, a joyful call to holiness and to union with him through her intercession and our response.

"I call on each one of you to decide consciously for God and against Satan. I am your Mother and, therefore, I want to lead you all to complete holiness. I want each one of you to be happy here on earth and to be with me in heaven. That is, dear children, the purpose of my coming here and my desire" (5/25/87).

PART 2

Dear children
I invite you
to pray with your hearts.
The Lord wants to
cleanse you of sin.
You need my help;
you can't do it alone.

Thank you
for hearing my call.

PART 2

Living the Messages

So we come to the heart of this book. In this section we will be reflecting on five specific areas of our Lady's messages: Eucharist, prayer, fasting, Scripture reading, confession, and conversion — evangelization.

As we engage each topic, we will share with you some ways in which we are trying to live the messages in our lives and the discoveries we have made along the way. It is our hope and prayer that in sharing these often very personal pilgrimages of the heart we will help you to realize that the Gospel message as reflected in our Lady's words at Medjugorje is not an impossible dream but a graced possibility for all of God's children. It is obedience to the will of our loving Father. It is sharing in the redemptive life of our brother and savior Jesus Christ. It is opening ourselves to the unlimited power of the Holy Spirit. Mary asks all of this from us as she appears on the hill and mountain and in the church.

"Dear children, I invite you to be an example to others in everything, especially in prayer and testifying! Dear children, I cannot help the world without you. I want you to cooperate with me in everything, even in the least things! So dear children, help me that your prayer may come from the heart and that you all may give yourselves up to me completely! In this way I shall be with you. Thank you for hearing my call" (8/28/86).

CHAPTER 6

Eucharist

The Eucharist was the center and focus of all my (Father Ruane) pilgrimages to Medjugorje. Though my experiences at Apparition Hill and the Mountain of the Cross were certainly blessed, the Mass at Saint James Church was where all the threads of what God was doing through his Mother were drawn together in a special way.

The evening Mass is always said in Croatian. There are usually so many priests and people there from other countries that the Gospel is always proclaimed in at least two or three other languages. The first part of the Eucharistic prayer is said in Latin so that all priests can share in that very vital part of the Eucharist.

The singing in the church at Medjugorje is memorable because of its fervor, enthusiasm, and beauty. It is amazing how those melodies and a few of the Croatian words became so deeply impressed in my mind that often at home I would hear myself singing or humming them. Occasionally I would hear that beloved music as I was celebrating Mass at home, which was a lovely connection with those worshiping so far away from me in New Jersey. At all times these snatches of her music come as special gifts from our Lady to remind me of her messages and her love.

Mary and the Eucharist

Every Marian shrine which I have visited has always had the Eucharist as the main focus or certainly one of the main focuses. An Irish priest friend of mine has a delightful explanation of the way Mary serves Jesus at Lourdes: "When dawn comes and the Masses begin and go on throughout the day, our Lady points the pilgrims to her Son in the Eucharist. She reminds all of them most forcefully that he is her Lord and our Lord, her healer and our healer. Later in the afternoon there is Eucharistic adoration and the blessing of the sick with the Monstrance. Then at dusk Jesus hands the shrine over to our Lady as the rosary begins, with the processions and the famous Lourdes hymn. He asks his Mother to care for the sick and all who attend them throughout the night until once again they return to his Eucharistic presence as dawn arrives."

In some way the same thing is true at Medjugorje where Masses in many languages are celebrated during the morning. In the evening service the ten decades of the rosary plus hymns and prayers precede the main Eucharistic celebration, and then the thanksgiving service is another hour of prayers which contain the glorious mysteries of the rosary and special prayers for healing. We will speak much more about healing later on, but please notice how the healing prayers at Medjugorje are in the context of giving thanks for the Eucharist. The glorious mysteries of the rosary lift our minds, hearts and bodies to the realm of victory, power, and eternal union with God.

After Mass all religious items are also blessed. What a beautiful and intimate connection! Our Lord in the Eucharist, and our Lady by her rosary accompany each and every religious article blessed at that time. We who have been pilgrims to Medjugorje might want to explain this special connection when we present our gifts to relatives, friends, and co-workers. I believe they will feel doubly blessed if we do.

Another memory of Eucharist at Medjugorje is the fervor of the people who gather there two or three times a day to celebrate Eucharist. Both the villagers and the pilgrims who attend are there because they want to be. The conditions are often far from the best because most of the time a huge number of people are jammed into the church. Many other times it's either too hot or too cold to be comfortable. And over two-thirds of the people are generally standing.

I am always deeply touched by the faithfulness and attention of the people who are often suffering from jet lag, fatigue, and other ailments, but who nonetheless come and stand for hours at a time to be able to celebrate the Eucharist and receive Communion. As a priest, I have been privileged to have a seat at every Mass and I am aware that that is a great blessing.

Celebrating Mass in Medjugorje

More importantly, as a priest I have been privileged to celebrate the main English Mass at 10:00 in the morning. Also I have celebrated Mass in the Apparition Room, the small former sacristy off the sanctuary where our Lady appeared for several years. At other times I have been a concelebrant at both the English morning Mass and the Croatian evening Mass.

Each experience has been blessed although I do prefer to be the principal celebrant either in the church or in the Apparition Room. There is an active involvement when I am principal celebrant which energizes me and focuses my attention. There's also a spiritual communication that goes on between the priest celebrant and the people which, to me, is very special.

Since I don't understand Croatian (although I am learning more words and phrases) I find it difficult to sit through a homily that goes for twenty to forty minutes. Frankly, that long a homily would be a challenge at any time or any place, no matter what the language. In Medjugorje the priests preach at great length and so I have come to see it as a challenge to pray with the priest and for his anointing to say what our Lord wants him to say. It is an opportunity I use to pray for many special intentions and at times I have prayed part of the rosary for the peo-

Father Ruane celebrates Mass in St. James.

ple gathered there. My prayer is always that all of us, no matter what our language or national difference, will sense in the unity of the Spirit that we are called to be God's beloved children and that, in fact, is what we are in Christ Jesus.

Distributing Communion

I have always loved the Eucharist. It is actually the reason for my priesthood, so I was destined to enjoy celebrating Eucharist at Medjugorje. Helping to distribute Communion is a special joy to me, no matter whether it is to a small group of people, to a regular church congregation, to over six thousand people at the Nassau Coliseum for the Tri-Diocesan Charismatic Conference of Greater New York, or to some of the three hundred thousand people at the Eucharistic Conference in Bombay in 1964.

I do definitely prefer small groups, and so at Medjugorje I had to dampen my wild Irish temper, which got annoyed with the crush of people wanting to receive Communion. Then it dawned on me that I needed to make a quick act of repentance for that reaction. Then I could proceed in love to give Communion to these sisters and brothers who were literally hungering to receive the Lord. What right did I have to demand proper decorum and all that nonsense when there was a sea of people longing to be fed?

Sharing a Family Meal

The image that has helped me is some of our large family gatherings when we all finally sit down to share a meal. There is laughter and talking and movement and it definitely isn't a formal occasion; but it's a very special occasion. I treasure those memories of family gatherings and I treasure the memories of God's family gathering for Eucharist in Medjugorje. And I thank God he gave me the grace to repent of my impatience, and learn how to love in deed as well as word.

The Centrality of Eucharist

All of the visionaries agree upon how important the Eucharist is. Ivan said that for the last nine years the Eucharist has been the most important thing in his life and that he has never missed going to Eucharist except for the most serious reasons, such as sickness, travelling, etc. Maria has also said the Eucharist was the focus of her life and nothing is more important than daily Mass. It is the central, principal, essential activity of her Christian life. In fact, when someone asked her if the daily apparition of the Blessed Virgin Mary was the most important part of her day, she responded, "No. The most important part of my day is going to holy Mass."

In 1985 our Lady said to all of us, "You do not celebrate the Eucharist as you should. If you would know what grace and what gifts you receive, you would prepare yourselves for it each day, for an hour at least. . . ."

Recognizing that importance, the priests and people of the parish not only participate at daily Mass but have an hour of preparation before the main evening Mass when they pray and sing together. There are also certain definite times for adoration of the Eucharist — an hour on each Thursday and two late evening services at 10:30 on Wednesday and Saturday.

The parish staff has just recently finished a new chapel for adoration of the Lord in the Eucharist. What a blessing it will be to have a place set aside for silent prayer in the presence of the Lord.

The Tabernacle Wall

In November one of the pilgrims asked me if I would do her a favor and check to see if there were a picture of Jesus on the inner back wall of the tabernacle. I replied, rather off-handedly, that no one would put a picture there because who would ever see it? However, as the doors of the tabernacle are left open during the distribution of Communion at Medjugorje, I thought it just might be possible. So I looked and there was no picture there.

The person (and several others on my four pilgrimages so far) said she saw a picture of Jesus on the back wall. What I said then, I would say again. "That's a special gift to you and obviously is meant to reassure you that Jesus is truly present in the host we receive and in the host we venerate and adore at Benediction and holy hours." Deep down I wish I had seen that picture as I could use a little nudge to my faith. I do believe but, Lord, help me to believe even more with or without pictures in the tabernacle.

On May 28, 1990, I celebrated the 30th anniversary of my priestly ordination. Someone gave me money for a trip and I chose to go back to Medjugorje with another one of my three sisters (that leaves me only one more sister to take with me on pilgrimage). We arrived the Friday before Pentecost and stayed for five days. Once again the Eucharist was a special time for me.

My Pentecost Pilgrimage

On Pentecost Sunday I was asked to be one of two concelebrants who wore red vestments and flanked the principal celebrant. I must admit that I was delighted at the recognition of my anniversary but, most of all, by the honor paid to the priesthood. The other concelebrant was from Canada and had been ordained twenty-three years that day. Father Phillip Pavish, OFM, from Saint James' staff, was the principal celebrant and was celebrating his thirty-third anniversary. That's eighty-six years of service to the Lord and his people and a good cause for celebration. But there were forty or fifty other English-speaking priests there with hundreds of years of combined service and that was an even greater reason to rejoice and honor Jesus, the Great High Priest.

The previous day a priest from Malaysia had been principal celebrant. Ordained only ten months, he actually glowed, bubbled, and almost did a jig because of his joy at being the principal celebrant of the Mass. I hope you get the picture. This was a priest who loved what he was doing and he received a tremendous round of applause at the beginning when he told the congregation how young a priest he was, and another round of applause at the end when he told them, "I love you all."

Some pilgrims from my group were deeply moved by the whole incident. One of them said, "That's the first time any priest ever told me he loved me at Mass." Maybe more of us priests might want to share every once in a while our feelings of love and affection for our people.

Because of the number of English-speaking priests who were present in June, Father Phillip, the Franciscan in charge of English-speaking pilgrims, had begun to ask one priest to be the principal celebrant and another to preach the homily. The Malaysian priest was paired with an Australian. Actually each of them thought he was to be the principal celebrant and so they and their pilgrims were prepared to minister at the Mass. Calling on the wisdom of Solomon, Father Phillip refused to decide and left it up to the two of them.

The Australian hesitated for a few moments, but not the Malaysian, who scooted home by saying, "I'll be the principal celebrant, you preach!" There was a beautiful peace about the whole decision as the Australian priest yielded graciously and generously and did honor to himself and his whole continent.

I have characterized my fourth pilgrimage to Medjugorje as a celebration of Pentecost and the priesthood and its various aspects. Each day, of course, was a celebration of the Eucharist; and each also celebrated some aspect of priesthood.

Celebrating the Priesthood

Our group went up to Father Jozo's parish in Tihalijna. We began the day by praying the rosary on the bus and then again with Father Jozo in the church. We prayed for all priests and for many more priestly and religious vocations. Father was very much aware that we two English-speaking priests were celebrating our anniversaries. Two Italian groups joined us for Mass and their priests concelebrated also.

At the end of Mass, Father Jozo asked that a beautiful meditation on the priesthood be read in both English and Italian. Then he called up a couple from our group who were celebrating their 30th wedding anniversary on that day. All five of us priests prayed a special blessing upon them. Father Jozo asked me to conclude the prayer in English. Then he asked if we priests would pray over him. Afterwards, he invited all of the pilgrims, about 125 of them, to come up and be blessed by the four of us as he himself had to leave.

Because I have been in the healing ministry for a long time, I have no reluctance to pray over people. The other three, especially the two Italians, needed some encouragement. But they joined in readily and prayed beautifully with the pilgrims. What I especially liked was that people from the various language groups felt free to go to any priest.

The emphasis on priesthood at Pentecost '90 in Medjugorje convinced me that we need to celebrate priesthood more and more. In fact, one person was encouraging me to celebrate my 30th anniversary with as much fanfare and solemnity as I could. He felt that it was most important that we honor the priesthood and those who have remained faithful to their calling since in the past twenty-five years so many people have been deeply disturbed by the number of priests leaving the active ministry.

When you return home from Medjugorje, most of the difficulties and inconveniences that you experienced at the Masses will be forgotten or at least will be far in the background. Normally what you will remember will be the joy of celebrating in a very special place the great act of love of Jesus Christ which is the Eucharist. You will, I hope, remember the singing and the tremendous enthusiasm of the parishioners and the pilgrims.

When you go to your parish church, you may miss those elements, but know that Jesus is there in his all-encompassing love. Enjoy the solitude and the quiet that your parish may offer you. Pray with your heart at the Eucharist and give thanks for the memories of Medjugorje, for the freedom to worship, and for the great gift of quiet and solitude which characterizes so many of our parish churches before and after Mass. But most of all join your thankful praise with Jesus in his great act of thanksgiving: the Eucharist.

* * * * * *

They Also Serve . . .

When Father says he was privileged always to have a seat at Mass, he wasn't kidding. One of the non-privileged, I (Sister Ruthann) stood and stood and stood all week through rosaries, Masses, adoration of the Blessed Sacrament. You name it, I stood through it. But, for the most part, it was not as awful as it sounds. Though I think that may, at least in part, be a function of my being tall. At least I could usually see the altar.

Eucharistic liturgies at Medjugorje are the heart and soul of everything that happens there. And, with one reservation which I shall deal with shortly, I found it exciting, even awesome to be in a crowd of people who were in church because they really wanted to be there, who were praying and singing and smiling at one another with real joy and an overwhelming sense of community. We were brothers and sisters in a special way, a good way, a holy way. Some of the communitarian sense was brought about by the pure crush of human bodies, but that didn't matter. What mattered was that we really were a community of believers. And I found that exhilarating.

People weren't just saying words; they were praying. And that's contagious in the highest degree! Home again and often in the midst of a "we-have-to-be-here-because-it's-Sunday" crowd, I try to recall that avid praying, that hunger for the Lord, and then I pray that feeling toward all those who are around me.

The reservation? Honestly, it was receiving Communion. Which I have to admit was not a prayerful experience. If Father thinks giving out Communion to a mob is trying, he should be **in** the mob. The fact is that some European and African cultures simply don't have a concept of lining up. It's not that they're rude. They just have a different way of being. A way that most Americans find very difficult to handle. And though I've been abroad often enough to expect it, I'm afraid it's something I'll never get used to.

So receiving Communion when I managed it (there were two days when I didn't manage it) was not the glorious experience I might have hoped for. At home, of course, it is quite different. Here I have the luxury of space which, for me, is much more conducive to prayer.

You, Lord, Are the Center of My Life

But to return to our Lady's words. She wants us to make the Eucharist the center of our lives. She says:

"When you go to Mass, your trip from home to church should be a time of preparation for Mass. You should also receive Holy Communion with an open and pure heart, with

St. James Church and the Rotunda

purity of heart and with openness. Do not leave the church without an appropriate act of thanksgiving" (10/84).

And she urges all of us to attend Mass daily. Now, I know all the excuses. I've used them. And the one I've heard most often is: "Our church only has a 7:00 (7:30, 8:00) Mass which is impossible for me to attend because of my work schedule." Which is probably true. But I think it's time for us to remember that **we are the church,** and if our parish Mass schedule is not serving its people, then the schedule needs to be changed. If it cannot, then we need to find a church, chapel, shrine, or retreat house which meets our needs for daily Mass. Our Lady knows how vital to our holiness is communion with her Son. "Mass is the greatest prayer of God. You will never be able to understand its greatness. That is why you must be . . . humble at Mass, and you should prepare yourselves for it."

And yet how casually we attend Mass and receive Communion, almost without thought. This incredible gift to us is so available that we often take it for granted. But, think. We are receiving the actual body and blood of Jesus Christ. Jesus, who is God! He loves us so completely that when he finished his human life here he was unable to leave us alone and wanting. He made it possible for us to come into complete intimacy with him every single day of our lives. A total union of God and creature. An absolute unity of the Divine and the human. No other religion on earth has been so gifted. Why are we not there?

If we are to live any of Mary's messages, we must live this call to reverence, love, and thanksgiving first. For it is only in the saving grace of Jesus Christ that we will find strength to live as we should. No, as we must!

The Eucharistic Prayer and the Universal Church

There is one more subject I would like to touch on here: the Eucharistic prayer. I have loved that particular part of the Mass for a long time as it has always seemed to me to be a very special love story about God and his relentless quest for our hearts, a story that comes to climax in the actual body and blood of Jesus on the altar.

I thought I would miss hearing it in English. But God had a gift in store for me. As I heard it prayed in Italian, in Croatian, in Latin, in French, in German, suddenly that incredible love story took on dimensions that I knew in my head but had not really felt in my heart. We are all of us his children, not just you and me or the people in my parish or the people of New Jersey or the people of the United States. As I say, I knew it; but until Medjugorje I didn't really know it in the best and deepest sense.

That prayer connected me to the universal Church in a mighty way. I felt oneness with the world in a special and very graced manner. And when, during the next week in Rome, I went to an Italian-cum-Latin Mass at St. Peter's, it hit me again: the universal Church so that "from East to West a perfect offering is being made." I remember, when I was a child, the nuns stressing that at every moment Mass was being celebrated somewhere in the world. The gift of Medjugorje is that now, at any moment, I can and do pause and join with that worldwide community of prayer in giving glory to God through our high priest Jesus.

I guess there are all kinds of ways to "receive communion." And this way, this communion with the Church, is one of the most awesome ways I have ever experienced. The next time you're at Mass, pay close attention to the Eucharistic prayer, that love story, and imagine it being told in a thousand languages to millions of people around the world. Then join me in deep thanksgiving that you and I are among those who can hear it every single day of our lives. Thank you, Jesus.

CHAPTER 7

The Rosary

"Today I call you to begin to pray the rosary with a living faith. That way I will be able to help you. You, dear children, wish to obtain graces, but you are not praying. I am not able to help you because you do not want to get started. Dear children, I am calling you to pray the rosary and that your rosary be an obligation which you shall fulfull with joy. That way you shall understand the reason I am with you this long. I desire to teach you to pray" (6/12/86). "Pray at least an entire rosary: joyful, sorrowful, and glorious mysteries" (8/14/86).

Our Lady has asked us to pray, pray, pray, and pray, and especially to pray the rosary. So let's talk about it and learn as much about it as possible.

Our Holy Father, Pope John Paul II, knows Mary's desire for a return to prayer and especially the rosary.

During an interview that he gave to a group of German journalists in 1980, Pope John Paul held up the rosary and said, "Here is the remedy against evil. Pray, pray and ask for nothing else. Put everything in the hands of the Mother of God. We must be prepared to undergo great trials in the not-too-distant future. Through your prayers and mine it is possible to alleviate this tribulation, but it is no longer possible to avert it. We must be very attentive to the prayer of the rosary."

* * * * * *

A Confession

First of all, a time for confession. I (Father Ruane) was brought up on the rosary as a young high school and college seminarian, but it was not a very stirring devotion. In the major seminary we had rosary devotions in October and May and on special feast days of our Lady. It was in the schedule and I prayed it with devotion as best I could.

As a young priest, I always carried several rosaries in my car and whenever I was driving members of the CYO any place, we always said it. They joked about it and complained about it, but prayed it devoutly.

After Vatican II and its emphasis on liturgical prayer, I gradually gave up praying the rosary except when the Dominican Sisters to whom I was chaplain had it on the schedule. I never tried to duck praying it, but never felt a great need to make it part of my private devotions. I had carried a rosary in my pocket for years in seminary and early priesthood, but now gave that up.

However, I always took it to bed with me at night just to have it as a companion, though I rarely prayed it. I often prayed it while I was driving. But in recent years I had downgraded even that in preference for praise songs and other prayers.

Back to Center Stage

Medjugorje brought it back onto center stage in my life and ministry. Now it is part of my daily prayers, and I would like to explain how I pray it, hoping that this information will help you.

I usually pray the rosary by starting off with a major intention and then I make one or more intentions connected with the moment in Jesus' life I'm praying about at each decade.

Certain mysteries are favorites of mine. The third Joyful Mystery, the Birth of the Lord, is one. I pray that the Lord will enter into my memory and be born with me so that if there are any memories of my birth process itself that are not positive and are not life-giving, the Lord by his birth will heal those memories. I also pray for those who are giving birth and for the children they are birthing that the Lord will bless and be with them in a very special way. I pray that fear will be removed and the mothers will be able to choose life. I also pray that the babies will grow to choose life and come to love life and to feel alive in new and special ways.

The third Sorrowful Mystery, the Crowning with Thorns, I offer for those who have mental illnesses and for people who care for them. I often pray at this time for the members of the Association of Christian Therapists (to which I belong) and for the Order of St. Luke and other groups of people who are in the healing ministry and/or the healing professions. We are called to alleviate the suffering of those who are physically, emotionally, and mentally ill who so need all the prayers they can get.

The third Glorious Mystery, the Descent of the Holy Spirit upon the Apostles, I pray for all bishops, priests, and deacons and for all leaders of Christian churches and all secular societies. Lately I have been adding a special prayer for pastors. They do not have an easy life. A friend of mine was made a pastor a few months ago and was sharing with me some of the problems and challenges that he was facing, especially with regard to personnel. He said, "Please, pray for me." I assured him that I would, and I do so at the third Glorious Mystery.

At this mystery I also pray for the Bishop of Mostar and the Franciscans of Medjugorje. There have always been disagreements between pastors and bishops but this is a particularly painful one. Yet our Lady seems to be saying that by prayer and fasting peace can come to the situation. She encourages all of us to pray for that, and so I do.

My Special Intentions

As an aid to your devotion, I would like to list some of the intentions that I pray for. Always remember that you yourself will have to personalize this particular approach to the rosary. Use mine, if you will, or use your own; but make each prayer, each mystery count.

The Joyful Mysteries

The Annunciation: Father God, help me to echo in my life the "Yes" of Jesus and his Mother to your will. Behold, I too am the servant of the Lord. Let it be done to me according to your will.

The Visitation: Jesus, care for all pregnant parents and bless all who go out of their way to help one another. Heal my mother and all my brothers and sisters and myself from any negative influences during the time of pregnancy.

The Birth of Jesus: Help me to say "Yes" to life, Lord Jesus, and to live it to the fullest. Heal by your love and birth anything that hurt me or others at the time of our births.

The Presentation of Jesus in the Temple: Strengthen my resolve to serve you, my God. Renew within me the graces of the commitment made at Baptism and renewed in Confirmation and many other times.

The Finding of the Child Jesus in the Temple: Jesus, give me a renewed and deepened love for you in the Eucharist and renew Eucharistic adoration in the Church. Bring many men and women to serve in the Temple of our day: your Church, O Christ!

The Sorrowful Mysteries

The Agony in the Garden: Jesus, help me to say and live my "Yes" to God no matter what the cost, even as you did when you said, "Not my will, but thine be done."

The Scourging at the Pillar: Help all who are addicted and especially those in 12-step programs. And bless all who are encumbered by low self-esteem. Let them be healed as they realize that you loved them so much that you accepted the terrible scourging and tearing apart of your flesh to save them.

The Crowning With Thorns: Bless all who suffer from mental illness and all who care for them. Guide and help all persons in the medical and health-care professions.

The Carrying of the Cross: Give me and all your followers strength to carry our crosses with you and for you. Teach us to grow through the crosses you allow to come into our lives. When I fall and fail, help me to follow your example and get right up again to follow you.

The Crucifixion and Death of Jesus: Lord, you died on the cross for me, in unspeakable agony. Help me to appreciate your loving sacrifice and the salvation it won for me. Lord, save your people from sin and evil and show me how I am to share in your work of salvation.

The Glorious Mysteries

The Resurrection: Help us to seek the things of heaven and to focus on them as our goal. Lord, by your cross and resurrection you have set us free; you are the Savior of the world. I claim the freedom you won for us.

The Ascension: God your Father lovingly received you in your full humanity back to your rightful place in heaven. Give me joy in your victory and your return to our Father God. Heal my relationship with my natural father, living or dead, and help all of us grow in love and understanding of each other.

The Descent of the Holy Spirit Upon the Apostles: Renew your church, its leaders, and bless all leaders of civil governments. Bless and renew our bishops, priests and deacons, and especially all those who pastor your flock. Heal the division between bishop and priests at Medjugorje and let them be one in proclaiming your goodness in sending your Mother to lead us to you.

The Assumption: Jesus, I pray for the healing of my mother and of all mothers in flesh, word, or deed. Bless all who will die today and all who have died. Where Mary has gone, we hope to follow. Strengthen our hope in your resurrection and our own also.

The Coronation of Mary as Queen of Heaven and Earth: I, too, Lord, want to honor and love our Mother Mary. Bless all who have heard and obeyed Mary's messages wherever and whenever they were given throughout this world: Guadalupe, Rue du Bac, La Sallette, Lourdes, Fatima, Medjugorje, Akito, and other places.

The Rosary Experience

When I started to say the fifteen decades of the rosary each day, I felt that it was not going to be easy. It has worked out fine, however. Most days on my way to the Institute offices I say the Joyful Mysteries, and on the way back I say the Sorrowful Mysteries. The Glorious Mysteries I say sometime in the evening. There have been times when I get to the end of the day and have not said any of the rosary, and then I have made the decision to pray the fifteen decades. Sometimes I use Father Slavko's book or another book. Most times I use the intentions I have just shared with you.

I also thought that I would be bored by the daily praying of the whole rosary. That has not happened because the rosary is really a meditation on the life of Jesus. As I centered on him, I discovered that he has a way of making things seem new. He also highlighted and reaffirmed the ABC's of what it means to follow him. He has reinforced the fundamentals in the repetitive and healing concentration on what he did for me and what he means to me.

It has not been boring. It has been challenging at times, but never boring. I remember being very, very tired one night and realizing that if I sat down I would fall asleep. So I walked around and knelt and prayed before my little Medjugorje shrine. It was a very blessed experience.

My prayer life has taken on a depth since going to Medjugorje. The first time I heard the message to pray the rosary. The second time it was ingrained in me more deeply during the beautiful retreat time that I had with the Lord and our Lady. The third time just confirmed that what I was doing was what God wanted me to do and also what I wanted to be doing. The fourth pilgrimage gave me a real desire to pray the rosary for priests and religious.

How blessed I feel to be able to meet the Lord each day in the rosary and relive the most important moments of his life! I pray that you will be blessed in a similar way and continue to grow in accord with God's loving plan for you.

Other Rosary Mysteries

Sometimes when I have prayed the fifteen decades of the rosary (Joyful, Sorrowful, and Glorious Mysteries), I add another group or set of mysteries. I often pray the Last Supper trilogy: (1) Jesus' institution of the Eucharist; (2) his institution of the priesthood; and (3) his giving us the great example of service by washing the feet of his apostles. Then I usually meditate for the fourth mystery on the adolescence of Jesus and his maturing in Nazareth during his hidden life. Finally I pray the fifth decade thinking about the public life of Jesus: his preaching, teaching, and healing ministry.

Other times I take one event or teaching and enter more deeply into it as I pray the Hail Mary's. Often I begin by reading a relevant passage from the Bible to set the tone of my prayers. I especially like to see how Jesus related to the various people in those moments, and at times I even imagine myself to be there, either as a participant or as a highly involved observer.

The Wondrous Mysteries

Someone in Medjugorje told me about the "Wondrous Mysteries" of the rosary, covering the stages of our Lord's public ministry. I will list them for you but must insist that this is an area for your own creativity to express itself. The Church has left us free to roam the Scriptures and to consider prayerfully the various times in our Lord's hidden and public life between the Finding in the Temple and the Agony in the Garden. Here are the "Wondrous Mysteries" as they were given to me.

1. Jesus is tempted by Satan in the desert
2. Jesus is baptized by John at the Jordan
3. The gathering of the disciples
4. The Beatitudes
5. The lessons and parables
6. The Golden Rule
7. The Lord's Prayer
8. Filling the fishermen's nets with fish
9. Feeding the multitude with loaves and fishes
10. Turning water into wine at Cana
11. Healing the sick
12. Walking on the water
13. Bringing Lazarus or Jairus' daughter back to life
14. Stopping the storm at sea
15. Jesus' triumphant entry into Jerusalem on Palm Sunday and his attack on the money changers in the Temple

Pray for Your Pastor

May I make a special request? In all your prayers, but especially in the rosary, please pray for your own pastors and priests. Pray for them by name. Perhaps you might pause at the name of Jesus and say, "Lord, bless Father. . . . Heal him. Be with him and love him."

I remember praying several years ago with a person who was in the Charismatic Renewal. She was a great friend of Father Patrick Peyton, but she didn't have much experience with the rosary and consequently did not use it. We happened to be driving into town one day to see Father Peyton and I said, "Well, let's say the rosary, but let's do it in a different way." We prayed the rosary with special intentions for each decade as I have mentioned, but also at the name of Jesus in each Hail Mary we prayed in tongues for those intentions. It was a very prayerful experience. The ride of almost forty-five minutes sped by so quickly that we were just coming to the end of the fifth Joyful Mystery as we pulled into the place where Father Peyton was staying. My friend remarked: "Thank you very much. I enjoyed praying the rosary that way. What a lovely experience and what a new insight that has given me."

Several times I have encouraged you to use your imagination as you pray with your heart. I believe that, as you do, you will be blessed in many ways and brought to a deeper understanding of God's will for you.

* * * * * * *

My Rosary "History"

My personal history with the rosary, once I (Sister Ruthann) stopped to think about it, amazed me. I mean, if you had asked, I would have acknowledged that, of course, the rosary was always there. But on reflection I realize that not only has the rosary always been there, it has always been

Pilgrims pray the rosary on Apparition Hill

alive in my life, though I can't claim I always viewed it as such. I can't even claim to have given it much thought at all.

As a child I found the rosary to be a real purgatory. It was soooo loooong, soooo boring, and the nuns (may they sit in God's lap forever) insisted that we say it soooo often. As soon as possible I escaped it, though as I have admitted more than once, I always carried a rosary with me, having been assured by those same nuns that the Blessed Mother got **anyone** who died with a rosary on their person into heaven.

When I entered the Dominican Order I found myself in a "hotbed" of rosary saying, tradition having it that the Lady gave the rosary to St. Dominic. At 4:45 every afternoon, come rain or come shine or come anything else, the rosary was prayed in our Motherhouse Chapel. I tried to like it. I really tried. But I failed. Perhaps it wasn't purgatory anymore, but it sure wasn't heaven either.

All Fifteen Decades?

Then in November of 1989 I went to Medjugorje and found out that our Lady wanted us not just to pray the rosary but to pray all fifteen decades! Every day! Oh, surely not. Couldn't I do something else instead? Anything else. But the messages were clear. Pray the rosary — the entire rosary — every day. So it really came down to: did I believe the blessed Mother was appearing in Medjugorje or not? Did I believe the messages or not? I had to say "yes" to both questions. Well then, argued my heart, if I believed it, was I going to do as the Mother of God asked or not? There really didn't seem to be a choice. I mean, if Mary showed up in my yard and asked me to pray the whole rosary every day, would I do it? Of course. Well, she hadn't shown up in my yard, but she'd made darn sure I'd gotten into hers. There didn't seem to be much room left for argument. Only for the rosary.

And so I began to do as she asked, to pray all fifteen decades every day. And I have to be honest, it was like an endurance test, something that had to be "gotten through," but certainly not something to be loved or enjoyed. However, I said to myself, in a way I'm getting double credit for this. I'm saying the rosary **and** doing penance at the same time.

That was ten months and approximately four thousand five hundred decades ago. Things are not the same. I've been deeply and wonderfully graced to love the rosary, to find it a prayer from the heart, to discover it as a center of peace in my life. But not all at once. As we know, healing is a process. And my healing vis-a-vis the rosary has been just that: a process, a pilgrimage of the heart.

Special Intentions

Along the way I've developed my own set of special intentions for each five decades and for each single decade. They have all become healing prayers as the praying of them has become a healing time for me and a time when I give great concentration to the healing of others, as my intentions will reveal. (I note parenthetically too that I no longer "say" the rosary, I "pray" it, and there is a marked difference.)

The Joyful Mysteries

I begin with the Joyful Mysteries and offer them for the healing of my family which has come to include Father Ruane, who is certainly among the best of my brothers. I pray it in total for all my family, including the ones who are not specifically named as I pray, living and dead, close and distant. I usually pray this rosary in the midst of my morning prayers and I have found that it is a most peaceful time for me, a quiet time of dawn and blessing for my family as the new day begins.

At the Annunciation I pray for Father Ruane that he will experience many angels bringing good news, that he himself will be the bearer of good news to others, and that he will be as faithful to his "yes" to God as Mary was. I visualize him there with her and the angels and pray for Divine healing in all areas of his life.

My mother is my primary intention as I pray the Visitation. I see her with Mary and Elizabeth, the three of them sharing their experiences of pregnancy and motherhood. And I pray that the healing presence of Jesus in Mary's womb will touch my own mother's pregnancies and heal any wound that she or I or my brothers or sister might have experienced while she was carrying us. I also ask Mary and Elizabeth to pray for and with her that she might always be blessed in her womanhood and her motherhood.

How I love praying the Nativity! It is so real to me, and I use this decade to pray for my sister, her husband, my brothers and their wives. I place each of them there with Mary and Joseph and the infant Jesus and watch, as I pray, as they interact with that holy family. I pray for their healing individually and for all of us as a family in the midst of that holiest of families.

The Presentation in the Temple gives me the opportunity to pray for my nieces and nephews. I give each of them, one at a time, to Mary and ask her to present them to her Son in whose presence may they always rejoice and find great love and healing. And I use the tenth Hail Mary, as I only have nine nieces and nephews at this moment, to pray for at least one vocation from among them.

The members of my immediate family who have died are my intention when I pray the Finding of Jesus in the Temple. Again, I name each one of them and pray that in death they will always be found in the Temple, in the presence of the Father. And I also ask them at this time to pray for me that I, too, may always be found — at least interiorly — inside the Temple curtain, worshiping.

The Sorrowful Mysteries

The Sorrowful Mysteries I offer for world peace as our Lady has told us in message after message to pray for peace. Again, each decade has its own special intention as well. During the prayers of the Agony in the Garden, I pray for the Mideast and the healing of the many divisions which are an agony on that holy ground and for all prisoners on death rows throughout the world. Africa is my intention, particularly the millions of refugees, as I pray the Scourging at the Pillar; and Russia and its satellite countries during the Crowning with Thorns. I offer the Carrying of the Cross for Central America and for all political prisoners everywhere; and Jesus's Crucifixion and Death for Ireland.

The Glorious Mysteries

I pray the Glorious Mysteries in general for all the people of the Institute: the volunteers, our benefactors, those who come to us for retreat, seminars, or private consultation seeking the healing of Jesus, and particularly for all those who have ever attended a Healing Mass.

The Resurrection decade I offer for all who will die that day that they may be admitted immediately into the joy of God's presence. And I offer the Ascension decade for religious unity, especially among Christians because the Ascension seems to be such a wonderful reunification of the Trinity. When I pray the third Glorious Mystery, the Descent of the Holy Spirit, I pray that the hearts of the world will be open to the presence of the Spirit, that conversion to holiness will happen among all peoples: political, social, economic, and ecclesial leaders and all those who have the ability to cause change — which, of course, includes all of us.

The Assumption of Mary I pray for those people who are presently coming to me for spiritual direction. And I usually tuck my sister, whose name is Mary, into this decade too. The Coronation of Mary I offer for all women, especially those in my religious community. I pray for their healing and for their own realization of the blessedness of their womanhood.

The Women's Rosary

I even have a rosary invention of my own. I call it the "Women's Mysteries." And I love it, not just because so much of my own ministry is with and for women, but because the stories it brings to my heart are so rich with healing messages.

I pray the first mystery in remembrance of Mary Magdalene's anointing of the feet of Jesus, and I ask her intercession that all women will be courageous enough to break open the jars of ointment they carry and let the gifts they contain pour out on the world.

The second mystery is what I visualize as the afternoon of Mary and Martha with Jesus. I pray during this that women may come to know and to embrace both the active and contemplative sides of their nature and to have strong and loving relationships with Jesus.

The woman at the well is the focus of the third mystery as I ask the Lord to bless all women with the challenge of knowing themselves and knowing themselves in him. I pray especially for those in troubled marriages that they might be healed and not have to suffer the terrible pain of divorce.

Or, if divorce becomes the most healing option, that the Lord will uphold them, strengthen them, and give them peace in that decision.

The fourth mystery I pray remembering the poor widow who gave "out of her need" to the Temple treasury and I ask the Lord to keep those women who have the ability to share mindful of those who do not.

The fifth mystery of my "Women's Rosary" is not scriptural but no one will ever convince me that it is fictional. It is the meeting of Jesus and his Mother following the Resurrection. I don't have a fixed intention for this mystery. Sometimes I pray it for mothers, sometimes for family reunification. And sometimes I am just so caught up in the joy and glory of it all that I simply pray for the happiness of praying it. I figure God will know what to do with whatever merit it might have.

What was once an ordeal has become a great gift. And I sometimes find that I have "finished" the prescribed Our Father and ten Hail Mary's before I have finished my heart's meditation on the mystery. So I just pause and continue to pray until I feel it is time to go ahead with the next decade.

But When?

Time. If you had asked me before I went to Medjugorje if I would have the time (not to mention the inclination) to pray fifteen decades of the rosary each day, and sometimes more, I would have said absolutely not. I don't have that much extra time in my day. But gently, oh so gently, as I prayed over the different messages from Medjugorje, I began to see where all that time was going to come from.

There is certainly a great deal of time in my car, time that I used to spend listening to the radio. There is time some evenings, time that I used to spend watching whatever flashed in front of me on television. There is more time in the morning. I simply moved my alarm back another fifteen minutes. There is more time than I know what to do with!

My Rosary Gift

Late in the winter just past I made a thirty-day retreat. And it was then, when I literally had nothing to do BUT pray, that Mary and her Son gave me the rosary gift I alluded to earlier. I am a poet, first and foremost, I think. And it was in my poetry that the gift was given. I wrote a series of poem-meditations on the fifteen mysteries of the rosary that are very special to me. I use them for my own meditation, and Father Ruane, who has read them, says he has used them as well.

Needless to say, praying the rosary is no longer a purgatory, no longer an endurance test, no longer something to be got through so that I can get on to something else. Instead I have found the rosary to be a most sacred encounter with Jesus, a way of being with him from that first incredible moment of Incarnation to the blessed time when he honored his Mother with Queenship. Yes, the rosary is a Jesus prayer because it centers on his life, death, and resurrection. It is also a Mary prayer: but as St. Bernard said, when we say, "Mary," she says, "Jesus." She loves him and us so much that she delights in bringing us together.

As I pray the rosary now I find myself growing closer and closer in intimacy to that One who emptied himself of his godliness to take on our humanity so that all of us could be enabled "to follow him more nearly, to see him more clearly, to love him more dearly." To love him whose name is simply Love.

CHAPTER 8

Pray Always and With Your Heart

"When you pray you must feel more. Prayer is a conversation with God. To pray means to listen to God. Prayer is useful for you because after prayer everything is clear. Prayer makes one know happiness. Prayer can teach you how to cry. Prayer can teach you how to blossom. Prayer is not a joke. Prayer is a dialogue with God" (10/20/84).

Vive La Difference!

Now we (Father Ruane and Sister Ruthann) would like to talk about other prayers which we love. You have no doubt become very aware of how different we are from each other. We are both extroverts, but in noticeably different ways, and that is true for so many other areas. Some of our differences are gender related while others have much to do with family and community relations.

We both come from big families which moved around a lot when we were young. Father Ruane has been a priest for thirty years while Sister Ruthann has just this year made final vows after nine years with the Caldwell (N.J.) Dominicans. Before that she had an active and varied life, both in business and the arts. As we continue to share, you may see areas of similarity as well as difference. We have been blessed by these similarities and differences in our ministry of healing as well as in the writing of this book.

* * * * * *

The Morning Offering

When I (Father Ruane) get up in the morning, I kneel by the side of my bed and say the Morning Offering.

"O Jesus, through the Immaculate Heart of Mary, I offer you all my prayers, works, joys, and sufferings of this day, in union with the holy sacrifice of the Mass throughout the world. I offer them for all the intentions of your Sacred Heart, the salvation of souls, reparation for sin, and the reunion of all Christians. I offer them for the intentions of all Bishops and all Apostles of Prayer, and in particular for the intentions of our Holy Father for this month."

And Other Prayers

Then, while showering, I pray the Apostles Creed and then say seven times the Our Father, Hail Mary, and Glory Be. Our Lady has asked us to say these prayers and I personalize them in this way. My mother is still alive, thank God, and I have two brothers and three sisters. I say one set of prayers for each of them and their spouses and children by name. Then I pray for the Sacred Heart Institute, especially for Sister Ruthann, and some of our very loyal volunteers: Fran, Elenore, Rosalie, Dorothy, and their families. So right then and there I have my seven particular intentions for those prayers.

However, I always want to pray in union with our Lady for all God's intentions and for her special intentions at that time. My intentions are secondary to God's and hers, but I know they hear and honor my love and concern for my family and the people of the Institute.

A friend mentioned how he prays for the souls in purgatory. He prays the Apostles Creed five times and then the Our Father, the Hail Mary, the Glory Be. He concludes by saying, "Eternal rest grant unto them, O Lord, and let perpetual light shine upon them. And may the souls of the faithful departed through the mercy of God rest in peace. Amen."

He also adds after each decade of the rosary the Fatima prayer: "O my Jesus, forgive us our sins; save us from the fires of hell. Bring all souls to heaven, especially those who have most need of thy mercy." And then he concludes with "St. Michael, the Archangel, protect us." I often conclude each decade with the short prayer: "Sacred Heart of Jesus, I place my trust in you."

The prayers we add at the end of each decade or each rosary are the "trimmings" on the rosary. Feel free to do something similar as such prayers make the rosary much more your own personal prayer than anything else. Enjoy yourself and be creative, spontaneous, and even playful with our loving God and his Blessed Mother.

The Apostles Creed

You may be wondering about the prominence given to praying the Apostles Creed and not just reciting or saying it. It is supposed to be our Lady's favorite prayer. She said, "The most beautiful prayer is the Creed." When I started saying the Apostles Creed many times, I thought it could be boring. But it wasn't. Rather it was a beautiful experience of going more deeply into what the Creed means. It is not just a series of statements about God (Father, Son, and Spirit). It is what I believe, what nourishes me. I was amazed and delighted at that realization and how special that prayer has become.

As you can tell by what I have written so far, I have been deeply touched by the message of Medjugorje. I have also had my prayer life expanded and blessed in a very lovely and holy way. My prayer for you is the following:

Lord Jesus, let the words of your Mother Mary at Medjugorje touch the hearts of your people. Renew them in their prayer life. Let them know that they are called to live with you, to talk with you, to be with you. Let their prayer be an intimate personal contact with you. Whatever form they use, bless it so that it will be a means by which you can speak to their hearts and they can speak to your Sacred Heart.

* * * * * *

Beginning the Day

I (Sister Ruthann) have learned literally to begin my day with prayer. When I first come to consciousness in the morning I say, "Good morning, God. Thank you for keeping me safe during the night and for the gift of a new day in which to serve you." I say "learned" because prayer is a habit like any other. You do it and you do it and you do it some more and again until it is almost automatic.

Then I make the sign of the cross, say the Glory Be, and only then do I get out of bed. But I get out smiling because I know that my day is already safely put into the hands of God.

Holy Smorgasbord

I'm not going to give you a litany of each moment of my prayer life. But as I try to pray more and more, God has uncovered some ideas for me which I happily share with you. So welcome to my "holy smorgasbord." Take what you want, leave the rest. And when you get some prayer ideas that haven't occurred to me, please, let me know what they are!

Official "prayer times" are more than important. They are vital. They are food and drink for our souls as surely as breakfast, lunch, and dinner are for our bodies. And we can starve our souls to death as surely as we can our bodies. May our gracious God ever preserve us from anorexia of the soul! But these official times are when we close the door, put out the "do not disturb" sign, turn off the volume on the telephone, and spend time in dialogue (not monologue) with God. We speak to him. We listen to him. And we do not let **anything** interfere. It doesn't matter when during the day we do this. We all have our own schedules to deal with. But it does matter that we do it. Oh, it matters very much.

Then there are all those other times. As I discovered when I set out to pray all fifteen decades of the rosary each day, there is more time than I ever imagined! All those little pockets of time I have discovered in my day. Not large enough for a rosary, but more than ample for a small prayer or two: waiting at the gas station, standing in line at the grocery store, boiling water for tea, combing my hair, making the bed.

The list is probably endless. Think of all those things we do, or those minutes we wait, which now are really wasted time. Our bodies may be busy, but our minds aren't. Mary showed me that "free" time and then showed me that a prayer doesn't have to be long and involved and intricate. It can be a quick "Sacred Heart of Jesus, I place my trust in you." Or even, "Hi, Jesus. Just checking in to let you know I'm thinking about you."

So now I pray at every available moment. Little prayers. Big prayers. Medium-sized prayers. Prayers for love. Prayers for peace. Prayers for holiness. Even, right at this moment as I type the manuscript for this book, prayers for you who will read it. It's a wonderful way to live because it colors my whole day with the radiant pigments of God.

St. Paul says, "Pray always." And I puzzled about that for years. How could I possibly pray **always?** I mean, there are many, many times — in fact, most of my waking time — when my mind is engaged. And when I'm asleep I'm not even aware or in control of that mind. How could I pray then? Well, a couple of years ago, long before I ever even thought of Medjugorje, I heard the expression, "Pray with the heart." If I'd been a cartoon character a light bulb would have gone on over my head, because suddenly I knew how I could pray always.

Praying Always

There are two constants in my life, two things that happen and will happen as long as I live. One is my breath, the other is my heartbeat. So now each morning when I awake and each night as I go to sleep, I offer these two things for whatever intentions I most want to pray for. And I know that Jesus, Lord of my waking and my sleeping, accepts that offering, that twenty-four-hours-a-day activity; and in his hands it becomes the prayer I desire it to be.

There is no moment that cannot be a prayer if we listen to our Mother at Medjugorje, especially there is no moment that we cannot be praying with our hearts.

CHAPTER 9

Fasting

The best fast is on bread and water. Through fasting and prayer, one can stop wars, one can suspend the laws of nature. Charity cannot replace fasting. Those who are not able to fast can sometimes replace it with prayer, charity, and a confession; but everyone, except the sick, must fast'' (7/21/82).

Well, there you have it. One thing about our Lady is that she's quite clear about fasting as an important part of her five-point plan, her message.

I (Father Ruane) personally have never found it easy to fast on bread and water except when I am on retreat. Bethlehem Hermitage in Chester, New Jersey, is a favorite place for me when I go on retreat. Each Wednesday is a day of complete solitude and fasting. At the end of the morning Mass, Father Romano blesses a loaf of bread and presents it to each hermit or visitor. Then he anoints the person and prays that God will use the fast in a special way.

Being the type of person that I am, I immediately, upon returning to my hermitage, divide the bread into four portions. I use three for my meals and the fourth and smaller portion for a snack in the evening so that I don't go to bed hungry. God gave me my personality and its analytical approach, so I think I honor him by being prudent and planning well.

Fasting at Medjugorje

Fasting at Medjugorje is not a tremendous problem except when I find myself in the position of not wanting to offend the local host family by refusing a simple meal prepared with great hospitality. So while there I have usually broken my fast around 8:00 in the evening for dinner with the group. In the beginning many of the people at Medjugorje, though certainly not all, were fasting on Wednesdays and Fridays. And I'm certain that some still do. But that does not prevent them from providing a very substantial meal for their guests!

One day when I was fasting one of the sister sacristans allowed me to use the restroom in the rectory and then said, "Why don't you stay for some tea?" Well, the tea was accompanied by some cakes. I finally settled on some apple cake, it being the closest thing I could find to bread and it's my favorite anyway. In the midst of my inner dialogue, I felt the Lord say, "Please, you don't have to make excuses. Charity comes before fasting; and you can even fast from fasting when the occasion arises."

I like our Lady's emphasis on the importance of fasting. It's an integral part of her message and she mentions it frequently as a way toward holiness.

The best fast is on bread and water, as she says. One priest commented on that by saying that the bread and water in Medjugorje are much better than the normal bread and water in the United States. My response to that is to make sure you get good bread and very good water. I do think that our Lady is asking us to be serious about making fasting a part of our lives, though I don't think we should get scrupulous about it. She has suggested that we also fast from alcohol, drugs, TV, and — I might add — from smoking or any other practice which could be harming us.

Giving Glory to God

Fasting is a penitential practice by which we glorify God rather than self. We say **yes** to God, and **no** to self, to excess, and perhaps even to sin. Sin is saying **no** to God and **yes** to self. Sin is saying me, me, me, rather than concentrating on Thee, Thee, Thee. When we sin, we glorify self and not God. I have put fasting and sin together deliberately so that it becomes obvious that fasting is important, not just a whim on our Lady's part, but a very real concern and a healing corrective to sin and its influence in my life and possibly yours also.

Jesus fasted in the desert and at other times. Christians for centuries have fasted as a penitential practice. Over the centuries we have reduced the practice to nearly nothing, and now the Lord is telling us through his Mother to get with the program again.

If you find fasting on bread and water impossible, I would suggest that you do it for a few hours on Wednesday and Friday. And for the rest of the day, be very moderate in your use of food. Why not prepare and eat only simple foods?

One Lent when I was chaplain to the Caldwell Dominicans, the sisters decided that they would have soup and bread for their main meal on Wednesdays. I thought it was a good idea because the money we saved was going to be given to the poor. The cooks made homemade soup and homemade bread and, I have to tell you, it wasn't a great sacrifice! It was a very simple meal but quite nutritious and enjoyable. Let simplicity be a part of your approach to fasting.

I do encourage you to do it as our Lady requests when it is possible. Be prudent, however, and if your fasting becomes a cross to your family and co-workers, then modify it. But don't give it up completely. My concern is that in our perfectionist approach, it's either all or nothing. I suggest in our society and our culture that we be prudent, persistent, and willing to grow in this practice. I have followed this approach and find that fasting is becoming, if not easier, then at least less stressful.

Sharing in the Cross

I must tell you that at times I feel perfectly justified in giving up the fast for any number of reasons. Charity is the primary one. Another one is when I become aware that I have become a bear and quite obnoxious because I'm fasting. My theology says, as I mentioned before, that fasting is supposed to help me share in the cross of Christ. It is not meant to force others to bear the cross because of me and my attitude.

There are several reasons to fast. One is to comply with our Lady's request. Another one is to learn to control our desires and our hungers. A third one is to be able to share some of our resources with those who are in desperate need of them. Whenever we're hungry or our stomachs start to growl, it is good to remember that there are people hungrier than we are and they don't have a choice about it. We do and we can go the extra step and send some money to them through Catholic Relief Services, CARE, or any number of other groups.

Other Ways to Fast

One other form of fasting that our Lady recommends is from TV. I've done enough research in the writings about 12-step programs to realize that watching TV can be a great temptation for almost every addiction. In one way or another, it reinforces addictive behavior or, as the expression goes, feeds one's addictions. This is true for alcoholics, sexaholics, overeaters, drug abusers, gamblers, whatever.

Our Lady has said that when we turn off the television set, the images remain in our minds. In fact, they occupy quite a bit of our thinking either at the conscious or subconscious level.

Television and movies have great power. There is an added dimension to their impact because they are even more attractive, seductive, and influential than real life. So fasting from TV is not only good as part of our Lady's overall plan, it is also good from a personal perspective as well.

We are social beings and so I find I fast better when I am with a group of people who are sharing that fast. We support and encourage each other by our very presence together and by our prayers which are a wonderful substitute for a big meal.

* * * * * *

Life Is Good!

My (Sister Ruthann's) spirituality is definitely **not** one of mortification. God gives lavishly and I take lavishly. I love life and all the good things and people in it. I love crunchy red apples and pungent cheese and oh! do I love chocolate. And I think it makes God happy when he sees us enjoying all his delights.

Maybe I'm just lazy. Maybe I'm too self-indulgent. I've been called both at one time or another, actually several times or another. But the truth is that I don't believe at any level of my being that God did such a splendid job on the world so that we could turn our backs on it.

So when I got to Medjugorje and heard about "bread and water," I was not pleased. Not even a little bit. But if our Lady says it, then I'd better do it, at least as far as I am able. But as I have pursued the great "fast ideal," sometimes failing miserably, I have begun to see a poetic beauty about it that is still very much in line with my idea of the spiritual.

Rediscovering the Gift

Fasting is not giving up something because it is bad or because I don't want it. Fasting is not saying to God, "No, I can do without your gifts. Thanks anyway." Just the contrary. Fasting has opened my eyes (not to mention my stomach) to appreciate these gifts even more. In deep and holy ways I rediscover them and I sharpen and rediscover my own senses as well. It's not really a punishment. In fact, it's another gift.

Our souls hunger for big things, for powerful motivations; so I find that I am more successful in my fast if I offer it for a very specific intention. It makes the fast "for" something instead of "against." Please, understand me when I say that I have not got fasting down to what my nephews would call "easy-peasy-lemon-squeezy." But if I fast in the context of prayer and for an important reason, it becomes more bearable.

A couple of months ago a friend of mine went to Medjugorje. I felt that his pilgrimage was a needed one, that something was pulling him there, and that there was some special grace in store for him. So I fasted for him for the entire week that he was gone. It was the easiest fast I've ever done.

Little Fasts

And, just as with prayer, there are all kinds of "little" fasts that we can do throughout our day. We can fast from fifteen or thirty minutes of sleep in order to pray. We can fast from having a cigarette right now and deliberately wait a half hour or an hour before satisfying our craving. We can fast from desserts, from coffee, from alcohol, from potato chips! We can fast from almost anything. Gloriously and with God's help, we can fast from sin.

Most certainly I agree with Father that we can fast from television . . . and from most modern novels . . . and R-rated movies, none of which are specifically designed for our salvation. I can't remember what the actual figures are for television watching in America. But my guess would be that it's at least three hours a day. Multiply that by seven and you have twenty-one hours a week of watching programs, most of which — though not all — present sin as the norm, as a joke, or a harmless diversion. Whether you're addicted to something or not (and most of us are addicted to **something**), the great bulk of television programming promotes sin and undesirable behavior. Twenty-one hours a week of television. One hour a week of church. It's pretty easy to figure out who wins.

We can, in fact, fast from any unnecessary and/or self-indulgent behavior. But, please, don't turn your life into a hair shirt. Anything, even a good thing, can be done to excess. Enjoy the wonderful things our gracious God has given us. Enjoy them by giving them up for a time. And enjoy them by using them too.

Just one thing more. Do remember to say, "Thank you."

CHAPTER 10

Confession

"Confession should give an impulse to your faith. It should stimulate you and bring you closer to Jesus. If confession does not mean anything for you, really you will be converted with great difficulty" (11/7/83).

"Today I wish to call you all to confession, even if you have confessed a few days ago. I wish that you all experience my feast day (The Annunciation) within yourselves. But you cannot experience it unless you abandon yourselves completely to God. Therefore, I am inviting you all to reconciliation with God" (3/24/85).

A Call to Repentance

Many people in Medjugorje experience a call to celebrate the great sacrament of Penance/Reconciliation, to go to Confession. Most people sense that celebrating the sacrament will be the seal of their Medjugorje pilgrimage. For many, it is just that as they experience the great all-encompassing and forgiving love of Jesus, as they respond in faith to God's grace, they feel the cleansing power and healing presence and forgiving love of Jesus. As they respond in faith to God's grace, they feel the cleansing power and healing strength of that great sacrament by which we encounter Divine Love through the ministry of a brother priest.

At Medjugorje in the summer it is not unusual to have seventy to one hundred priests spread out around the church celebrating the sacrament of reconciliation with pilgrims from all over the world. On a recent pilgrimage, within one hour, I (Father Ruane) was blessed to be the Lord's minister of peace and healing with people from various parts of the United States, Australia, Ireland, Singapore, and other places. What a blessing and a thrill that hour of divine mercy was to me and, I trust, to them.

Celebrating the Sacrament

Each time I have been to Medjugorje I have celebrated the sacrament with a brother priest because of the holy place I was in and because I like the sacrament and try to celebrate it monthly. In February my confessor was a young priest from Scotland who was the essence of gentleness and compassion. In April during Holy Week, I went to confession twice. The first time it was because of the tense and angry situation our group was experiencing. I wanted to be cleansed of any part I had in that situation; but more importantly, I wanted the grace and strength of the sacrament to help bring peace into my heart and to our group. The second time was on Good Friday when I was drawn to the sacrament as a way of repenting for all the sins of my life which had contributed to our Lord's suffering and death on the cross.

Some people do not work up the nerve to go to confession while in Medjugorje, but they often sense that something more is required of them when they return home. One person spent quite a bit of time in quiet prayer on Mount Krizevac after making the Stations of the Cross. He listened and responded to God's words of love. (What a great way to prepare for the sacrament!)

But he did not avail himself of the opportunity to confess. He came back to this country knowing that he wanted to do so here. Finally, when he felt the time was right, he did go to confession and was richly blessed. In some way his personal Medjugorje experience was unfinished until that moment. Something that had been left undone had now been completed and God has blessed him in new and deeper ways.

The priest who celebrated the sacrament with him was gentle, concerned, and very compassionate. He told him: "For your penance you should contemplate and consider how fortunate you are that Jesus has come to you in such a special way at this time in your life." He added at the end: "Listen very carefully to the Words of the Gospel [Mass was just beginning as he was confessing] as if they are being spoken directly to you."

For the young man these words were a great consolation and spurred him on to deeper conversion. Perhaps they may speak to your heart as they have most certainly spoken to mine.

Preparing for Confession

May I share with you some thoughts about the preparation for confession? Prepare yourself, please, by focusing on Jesus and his forgiving love. Ask him to show you what in your life he wants you to bring to this great sacramental encounter with him as saving Lord. And then do that.

It's wise to choose the right priest. If you don't know any of the priests in your parish or a neighboring parish, ask the Lord to direct you to the right one for you. Then be open to what the priest says because the Lord is working in him too, just as he is working in you.

While we were in Medjugorje for Holy Week, my sister Elenore met an eighty-four-year-old Dominican priest who was quite an amazing individual, going up and down Apparition Hill like a little leprechaun. When she felt our Lady's urging to celebrate the sacrament of Penance, she looked for him; but God directed her to someone else; and that someone else was the perfect confessor for her. Their celebration of the sacrament was a blessed occasion for both of them, but especially for her.

Wayne Weible tells the story of his own confession in **Medjugorje: The Message.**

> All day long — in fact, for the last several days — I had thought about going to confession. As a Protestant, this was new to me. We Lutherans had it publicly as part of our litany, but I was overwhelmed at the large number of pilgrims I had seen lining up inside and outside the church to go through this special sacrament. . . . As the cumulative impact of Medjugorje mounted, many pilgrims felt compelled to cleanse their souls through confession — some for the first time in years. By this act they would seal their Medjugorje experience in their hearts for the rest of their lives.*

Wayne finally gave in and went to a priest who was quite taken back by a Protestant wanting to go to confession. I'm glad to say both survived, though Wayne did not know which of them was more shaken by the encounter.

When you celebrate the sacrament in Medjugorje, it is as many people say, the capstone, the completion of your pilgrimage. But please, do not wait to celebrate the sacrament until you are in Medjugorje! Our Lady is calling us to regular (monthly) confession, so important is the sacrament for our spiritual growth.

Admittedly it is a lot easier to confess in Medjugorje because so many pilgrims are doing it and there always seems to be a priest available who speaks your language. It may very likely require more effort and planning to get to confession back home, but believe me, you will be really blessed by making that extra effort to celebrate the sacrament fervently and often. Our Lady has requested confession at pivotal times of the year in addition to regular times. She asks for confession before the new year,

*Wayne Weible, **Medjugorje: The Message** (Orleans, Massachusetts, Paraclete Press, 1989, p. 129).

Pilgrims line up for Confession at St. James Church

the anniversary of her first appearance at Medjugorje, and other times.

"Pray, pray! It is necessary to believe firmly, to go to confession regularly and likewise to receive Holy Communion. It is the only salvation" (2/10/82).

Please understand what our Lady is saying and do what she is asking in her ever so gentle and loving manner. Since my return I have tried to celebrate the sacrament each week. I don't get spastic if I go for eight to ten days, but I try not to let it go more than that. For I have always believed wholeheartedly in this sacrament and have been blessed in many ways by celebrating it often. Many of my best moments as a priest have been as a minister or recipient of the peace and reconciliation of Jesus.

May Christ, our compassionate and forgiving Lord, bless you with an understanding of this sacrament of his healing, and with a hunger to celebrate it with your newfound faith, according to our Lady's urging.

* * * * * *

The Resister

Whew! Now comes the hard part for I (Sister Ruthann) am both veteran and victim of the old "box." I could probably sit and trade horror stories with you for hours . . . which would accomplish nothing for either of us.

I am one of those who resisted confession in Medjugorje. I wanted to go. I even got in line once. But every part of me went into rebellion as I imagined walking back into a confessional box, dredging up all my dead bodies, and having some faceless priest give me some mindless penance and then slam the little door in my face while I was still making a "good act of contrition." Which is a good lesson in letting our imaginations run away with us. Since then I have learned from Father that the confessionals outside St. James are light and airy and open and the priests — probably inspired by the presence of the holy — are patient and kind and caring. But I didn't know that and, unfortunately, I wasn't able to hand everything over to God at that point. Such is the unhappy consequence of insisting on keeping "control."

Now, mind you, I have had some excellent experiences of confession in recent years with priests who were warm and loving and compassionate. But those boxes at Medjugorje were a hurdle I could not get over. I left feeling unsettled about it, wondering if I'd rejected some extraordinary grace. But life goes on, and it did, and so did I.

Other people were not so hard-hearted. One of our pilgrims celebrated (and I do mean celebrated!) the sacrament for the first time in seventeen years. Another told me she had gone, after having skipped over confession "for ages," because she figured it would be quick and easy given the lines of people waiting. Well, she said it **was** easy. But quick? Hardly. That priest, whoever he was, God bless him, spent almost forty-five minutes with her. And still another one told me that he had deliberately gone to an Italian priest because he figured the priest's English wouldn't be very good. Surprise! The priest was an American who spoke Italian. But the man told me it was one of the best confessions he'd ever made.

A Thirty-Day Retreat

Meanwhile, back with the repentant but stubborn nun in the United States . . . though confession was on my list of things to do, and though I did go to confession, I was still uncomfortable with not having gone in Medjugorje. It's funny, but I just couldn't get it off my mind. Something was wrong, off-center, incomplete, but exactly what that "something" was, I couldn't say.

When I made my thirty-day retreat in February-March, I figured confession would be part of the agenda; but I also figured it would be face-to-face and so perhaps, just perhaps, a really good experience. (My fingers are getting slower and slower on this typewriter. Some things are just hard to talk about, speaking of confession.)

The time for confession arrived and I couldn't get Medjugorje off my mind. Our Lady wanted something extra and she wasn't about to let me escape again. In fact, almost without my volition, I asked to make a general confession. Which I did. It's not pretty and it's not easy. But every time I faltered I would feel, actually feel, her presence around me, and I stumbled on.

The priest was, well, a miracle. For the first time in my life I experienced a Confession/Penance/Reconciliation as a gentle meeting of two sinners, loving and supporting one another, and both held tight in the embrace of Jesus. It was probably one of the holiest moments of my life.

Why am I telling you this? Because I know (oh, do I know!) how people resist going to confession. I know how painful and unsacramental it can feel. I know that all priests are not created equal and, humans that we are, we let that get in the way of what is really going on: an encounter not just with some tired and overworked priest, but an absolutely profound and intimate moment with God.

And I know too how cleansing and purifying and wonderful a moment it can be. To feel the no-strings-attached love and forgiveness of Jesus is to rediscover our innocence. And it is to be filled with new life, born into a fresh beginning, free from all that is stale and useless.

Things Will Change

When Mary says, "Go to confession," it is not because she wants us to wallow in our sins. It is because she knows that at confession, "the Holy Spirit comes, then peace will be established. When that occurs, everything changes around you. Things will change" (10/84).

Me? I could use some changes. So I'm going to keep trying to get to confession often, even if it means (shudder) that awful box. Because it isn't the box and it isn't the priest and it isn't even my sins that are the essence of confession. The essence is the Essence, the Essence of Life and Love and Goodness. That's what I pray for and I know that's what he is waiting to give me. . . . Whew!

CHAPTER 11

Scripture

"Dear children, today I call on you to read the Bible every day in your homes and let it be in a visible place so as always to encourage you to read it and to pray. Thank you for hearing my call."

One of the highest compliments I (Sister Ruthann) was ever given came from a woman who comes to me for spiritual direction. I walked into the room to meet with her and — because it was one of "those" days — I had left my Bible on my desk in my office.

"Oh," she said, "you don't have your Bible with you. You look different without it. I always think it's like your favorite piece of jewelry so you always wear it."

Wonderful words to hear, indeed. Because my Bible **is** something I "wear" all the time. On my person, certainly. But even more, in my heart. I love Scripture with a real passion. So there was at least one of our Lady's messages that I could affirm I was already doing. Thank God for graces given!

Finding Jesus

Scripture was, in fact, the second place I really **found** Jesus. (The story of the first place is long and doesn't properly belong here so it will have to wait for another time, another place.) It was a meeting ground for us, a place where I could listen to him, learn about him, and learn from him. It was simply a wonderful place to be.

So I would encourage you, as sincerely as our Lady does, to fast from words at least fifteen minutes a day to feast on The Word. I promise you, it's the best trade-off you'll ever make.

There is so much already written about praying the Scriptures (and there **is** a difference between reading them and praying them just as there is a difference between saying and praying the rosary) that I almost hesitate to throw in my nickel's worth. Almost. But not quite.

I was lucky when I first began reading Scripture seriously to have a guide, someone who said, "Read this" or "Try this." Because picking up a big fat Bible without a bit of a clue as to where to begin or how would be rather like trying to drive from New York to California without a map. You might get there, but it could take an awfully long time.

Unlocking the Mystery

So just for a minute, let me be your guide. Let me give you some clues to unlocking the mystery of the greatest love letter ever written: the Bible.

One good way to start is with the readings for the Mass of the day. Don't frown! I'm going to tell you how to find out. The priests of the Sacred Heart (Sacred Heart Monastery, P.O. Box 900, Hales Corners, WI 53130) put out a little paper flyer each month which tells you what liturgical week it is, what the readings are for each day, and what week of the Liturgy of the Hours is to be said. If you look at the Ordo (that's what the little flyer is called), and then at the contents page of your Bible, you should be able to locate the readings with a minimum of difficulty.

Sister Ruthann on Apparition Hill

Deciphering Bible shorthand is also easier than it seems. For instance, your Ordo might list a day's readings as follows:

2 Pet 3:12-15, 17-18
Ps 90:2-4, 10, 14, 16
Mk 12:13-17

The first reading is from the Second Letter of Peter (2 Pet), chapter 3, verses 12 through 15 and 17 through 18. The Responsorial Psalm is Psalm 90 (Ps 90), verses 2 through 4, 10, 14, and 16. And the Gospel is Mark (Mk), chapter 12, verses 13 through 17. On Sunday there will be one extra reading from the Old Testament. But that's all there is to it. That's one way to start and I think a very good way since it puts your reading into instant harmony with the universal reading of the Church that day.

Or, you could just decide to begin at the beginning with Genesis and read straight through till you get to Revelation (which is a particular favorite of mine). The only problem with that is that you will hit some less than fascinating reading right around Leviticus and parts of Numbers. So if you're going to do it that way, don't be daunted. Just skip over the more soporific passages.

Are you adventure oriented? Start with the Acts of the Apostles. It would make a great movie! If you prefer poetry, go to the Psalms (try Psalm 34!) or to Isaiah (especially chapter 55) or to John's Gospel (In the beginning was the Word . . .). Or, if you would like the comfort of the very familiar, begin with the Gospel of Luke. But whatever you do, begin!

Don't try to gobble the whole thing down at once. Remember, this is a leisurely healing journey with the God of the universe, not a forced march. Pick a short passage or one story and read it slowly and carefully. Then go back and read it again, this time relaxing your mind and heart so that God can do his work. As you read it the second time, perhaps a particular phrase will capture your attention. That's wonderful. Stop. And just savor the phrase. Odds are it's the particular word the Lord wants to speak to you today. Repeat the phrase to yourself slowly and gently. Let it take root in you. Ask the Lord to show you how it can apply to your life today. And always end by saying, "Thank you."

At various moments throughout the day, call the phrase back to mind. Give it a chance to become an important part of you and your day. And congratulations! You have begun to pray the Scriptures.

A second way to pray Scriptures is to begin as in the first method by reading through a story. Read it through a second time. Then put your Bible aside and imagine the story. Make it real. Put yourself in it either as a main character or as some character you invent. Interact with Jesus or Mary or the Pharisees or whomever the story is about. Don't be afraid to speak to them. And be certain to let them speak to you.

This is one of my favorite ways to pray the Scripture and a way I never tire of. It is always new and different and very, very healing to share part of Jesus' life with him and his family and friends . . . and even sometimes his enemies.

Taking a Chance on God

After you've been praying Scripture for a while, if you're feeling brave enough to take a chance on God, just open your Bible at random and let your eye fall on whatever passage it may. Trust that God has a message for you there and pray it carefully. Sometimes it may seem to be a very unlikely message, but if you relax your heart and mind and let God speak to you, I believe he will make clear to you what he wants you to know.

Our Lady knows better than any of us how eager her Son is to make us his own. And she knows that sacred Scripture is a very special meeting place. Listen to her words and invite the Word to come and make his home in you.

* * * * * *

The Bible Is Real People

I (Father Ruane) fell in love with Scripture long ago when I read the Book of Ruth and the story of Joseph's being sold into slavery in Egypt (Genesis 37 and 39-41). I marveled at how God rescued him from prison and made him the second most important person in the kingdom.

The Bible, especially the Old Testament, has always been for me these and other wonderful people — saints and sinners, prophets and sages, warrior men and women, peacemakers galore, and brothers and sisters responding to God's offer of love and protection. The Bible surely is the story of God's relationship with his people, but it's also the story of how those people responded.

Besides the beautiful loyalty of Ruth, the purity and astuteness of Joseph, there is David. As a shepherd boy he slays Goliath and as father-king he makes a mess of his children's lives. But through it all David loved the Lord his God and founded a kingdom which would last forever in his descendants.

In addition to these people, there are lovely passages from Isaiah and Ezekiel, Jeremiah and the other prophets, and the beautiful poetry of the Book of Psalms. There is the story of Jonah and the Song of Songs, so different and yet so truly inspired. There is love and hatred, loyalty and treachery, human cruelty and kindness. It's all so characteristic of human behavior that it will always, I pray, speak to me.

It all began in the garden with Adam and Eve and that blasted serpent. And don't forget Moses, Aaron and Miriam, and that motley crew they led out of Egypt. There is Joshua who led the desert-scarred and reformed people into the promised land, Joshua who proclaimed, "As for me and my family, we will serve the Lord." That's a sentiment we need more of today.

The New Testament

In the New Testament, Matthew, Mark and Luke are special but no one has ever touched my heart as John has in his Gospel and Letters and in the Book of Revelation. Despite the fact that many modern Scripture scholars believe that these books were written by followers of John, I still see the imprint of that impressionable young man who was so much the Lord's favorite, the disciple whom the Lord loved. What a man of love John was and how his love has lived on in so many of us as we seek to imitate his relationship with Jesus.

Another special favorite of mine is Peter. How I love that big-mouthed fisherman who was always the leader. I loved him when he proclaimed his faith in Jesus and when he denied him because of fear. How human a figure Peter is. What gifts of leadership and strength and how he needed the Lord to teach him how to get his act together. Three times he denied the Lord and three times he affirmed his love for that same Lord. Peter speaks to me in every fiber of my being as a follower of Christ to whom I can relate.

Now St. Paul was an entirely different story. I found it hard to relate to him. He seemed so blunt and even tactless at first. But then I reread the Acts of the Apostles and his letters, and behind that almost overbearing intellect, I glimpsed his love for Christ and his people, his tender regard for his companions —

The Chapel in the cemetery at Medjugorje

women as well as men. Paul may never inspire me as John and Peter do, but I'm thankful for his presence in my life. Slowly and carefully he and I are growing in friendship. That's a real blessing for me.

A Closing Prayer

Let's end this chapter with a prayer.

Jesus, Lord of Life and Word of God made flesh in our midst, teach us to love the Scriptures. Enlighten our minds and fill our hearts with a hunger for you and the details of your life and death. Help us to appreciate the long centuries of preparation for your coming and then their glorious fulfillment in your Person.

Mary, Mother of the Word, pray with us and for us as we accept your invitation to read the Scriptures prayerfully and often.

CHAPTER 12

Conversion and Evangelization

"Dear children, today I am calling you to decide whether or not you wish to live the messages which I am giving you. I wish you to be active in living and spreading the messages. Especially, dear children, I wish that you all be the reflection of Jesus, which will enlighten this unfaithful world walking in darkness. **I wish all of you to be the light for everyone and that you give witness in the light.** Dear children, you are not called to darkness, but you are called to the light. Therefore, **live the light with your own life.** Thank you for hearing my call" (6/5/86).

To appropriate the messages of Medjugorje for oneself, to hug them tightly like a well-kept secret, to seek salvation only for oneself is **not** what our Lady has in mind. We are to accept the light which we have been given and then let it be seen by all. As Jesus said, "Just so, your light must shine before others, that they may see your good deeds and glorify your heavenly Father" (Matthew 5:16).

Light. It is almost a Medjugorje theme. Lights on Krizevac, lights on Apparition Hill, the light of the sun dancing. And for this woman (Sister Ruthann), the light of a church tower glowing in the November night. The call is clear: be in the light, be of the light, and be the light for a world made dark by sin.

Baptized Into the Light

All of us who are baptized Christians are in the light. As we make our mature commitment to Christ, we become of the light. And some of us may find it relatively easy to be the light (at least some of the time) for our immediate world. I must confess to my own weakness, however; for very often fear of criticism or ridicule causes me to put a very thick and heavy shade on my own light. Do I really believe that "just a little" Jesus is enough? (Well, of course, it is; but you know what I'm getting at.)

Our Lady says, "I want you to be active in living . . . the messages." In other words, she is calling us to personal conversion. She wants us to give up old habits, old patterns of sin and laziness; she wants us to become light. Pray, fast, go to Mass and confession, read Scripture. But not in some rote or routine fashion. She wants us to do these things **with our hearts.** Only then, when our hearts are committed, will we be able to live the messages.

Live the Light

"Live" the messages, **live** them. That is the key word. Living is not something that we do in isolated or occasional moments or only when someone else is watching. Living is what we humans are doing all the time. Living prayer and fasting and Eucharist and penance and Scripture is what she is calling us to do. It is a challenge, a mighty challenge. But it is certainly not beyond the power of the Holy Spirit to work in us.

Truthfully, we wish it could be done all at once. But such is rarely the way. Conversion is a process, a healing process. And process involves time. As we convert, as we are healed, we are led closer and closer to the Light so that our own lights become brighter and brighter as we come nearer. Then we become, as our Lady says, "reflections of Jesus." It is in this reflection that we begin our work of evangelization.

I spent several of my growing up years in the South so I still shudder just a little when I hear the word "evangelize." In the Bible Belt evangelization too often meant people knocking on your door, leaving anti-Catholic tracts in your mailbox, under your windshield wipers, watching revival tents go up, and having absolute strangers harass you on buses about being "saved."

(One summer, I recall, my mother sent one of my little brothers off to a "Christian" day camp because it was the only one that had any openings. It all seemed to be going well until the evening he came home to announce that he'd been "saved" that day. My cute and very Catholic five-year-old brother had been baptized that afternoon because the minister demanded that anyone who wanted to go to heaven must come forward to be baptized. My brother wanted to go to heaven, didn't he? So much for "evangelization" of the more primitive kind.)

How Can We Spread the Good News?

At any rate, most of us are not yet comfortable doing the pavement pounding, doorbell ringing type of evangelization. What then? How can we live this injunction of Jesus and his Mother? I think our Lady's message contains the answer when she says, "Live the light with your own life." It is in example that most of us do our evangelization. And if we are really **living** the messages, we won't have to worry because our actions will speak clearly of what we believe and want to share.

What will probably happen then is that people will start asking questions. That is always so exciting to me, though

I must admit even I had to learn not to be bashful about answering. Jesus has said, "Knock and the door will be opened." When people come knocking, we must be prepared to open the door for them, just as others have opened it for us. Open the door, but don't shove them into the living room. Overkill can be as deadly as silence can. So temper your enthusiasm with prudence and gentleness. Speak the words our Lord and his holy Mother have taught you. And then let divine grace do its work.

Above all, pray. I remember once a woman speaking to me about a difficult situation in which she was deeply embroiled. She said, "The worst part is I can't **do** anything, just pray." And I replied, "Praying is doing something. In fact, it's probably the most important thing anyone can do."

* * * * * *

Being a priest for thirty years has enabled me (Father Ruane) to touch many people with the light Christ has given to me, with the light that he has asked me to be, to carry, and to share. I have preached every day at Mass since 1964, and sometimes two, three, or even five times on a Sunday. That's a lot of words and I am becoming even more aware of how easily they seem to flow from my lips and my heart. I do try to speak from the abundance of my heart (ex abundancia cordis).

Some Hesitation

For several years after I was ordained I hesitated to share much of my own difficulties in following the Lord. Somewhere or other I had absorbed the idea that I had to be the perfect priest. One of my C.Y.O. members even caught the idea and gave me a desk plaque with "Super Priest" written on it. You'll be glad to know that I got rid of the mistaken idea and the plaque about the same time.

I think it was in 1965 when I made a Cursillo de Cristianidad (Short Course in Christianity) and normally just called a Cursillo. Five of us priests were spending the three days and three nights with forty laymen, listening and sharing about Gospel values and how they affected where all of us lived and worked. I was awed by the sacrifices so many of the team and kitchen crew and the candidates had made to be there. They were evangelizing me and the other priests.

The Grace to Share

Since that weekend I share more about my personal living out of the Gospel in my life as a Christian person, a man, and a priest. I continue to focus on the Lord and his Word to us in the scriptural readings each day at Mass, but I am no longer shy about how I try and often fail to follow the Lord. People seem to appreciate what I say and especially my personal sharing. They tell me that they like my style of preaching better now. Some even remark: "Wow! You surely have changed." I make it a policy never to ask what I was like before! I'm just content to accentuate the positive and thank God for eliminating some of the negative in me.

I see my preaching and sharing, my writings and use of other media such as audio and video cassettes as my ministry of evangelization. Healing is often the best form of evangelizing as it makes people sit up and take notice of God and his call to repentance and reform.

One final thought. We, as a Church, are beginning to step out and share our faith by ringing doorbells and distributing literature about Christ and the Church. If you're asked to join a parish or diocesan committee on Evangelization, please pray hard and long before refusing. In fact, please do all you can to say "Yes." You'll learn many wonderful things about sharing your faith in Christ. What's even more exciting is that you will meet some wonderful brothers and sisters who are on fire for the Lord.

And it's catching. As the saying goes, "Faith isn't so much taught as it is caught."

Be part of the good news and keep the light of Christ alive and growing in today's world which needs it so much.

* * * * * *

Give Them the Light

"In your life you have all experienced light and darkness. God grants to every person recognition of good and evil. I am calling you to the light which you should carry to all the people who are in darkness. People who are in darkness daily come into your homes. Dear children, give them the light" (March 14, 1985).

So pray. Pray with your heart. Pray for conversion. Pray for light. Pray for strength to let that light shine no matter what the cost. Pray for us, please. And we will pray for you.

Come Holy Spirit and fill us with your grace and strength. Help us, in your glory, to renew the face of the earth.

CHAPTER 13

Healing and Medjugorje

As in all the places where Mary has come to her children, Medjugorje has experienced the extraordinary graces of many "signs and wonders." Mary wants us to believe:

to believe that she is there,
to believe in her Son, and
to believe and live the messages of Medjugorje.

But she knows the frailty of our hearts and the cynicism of our age; and so she, in the power of Jesus, gives signs and wonders to testify to her presence. Rosary chains have turned to gold. The sun has danced. Inexplicable lights have appeared on Mount Krizevac. We have seen these things ourselves and know them to be true.

And we have witnessed other miracles: the miracle of healing of the body, and most important, the miracle of the healing of the human heart, what we speak of as conversion. It is our intention in this chapter to devote our discussion to healing — physical, emotional, and spiritual — as these healings, more than any other signs and wonders, are the most frequent, the most well-documented, and the mightiest of the signs at Medjugorje.

* * * * * *

Stories Told and Untold

Someone recently asked me (Father Ruane) if there have been any healings at Medjugorje. I responded in the affirmative almost automatically because there are always healings and cures associated with shrines to the Lord, our Blessed Mother, and the saints. However, it wasn't until I began to do some research that the full extent of the healings at Medjugorje became apparent.

The Lord of all healing is doing a mighty work at Medjugorje. There are definitely many healings going on there and at other places because of its influence, because the messages of Medjugorje are having an impact on people everywhere.

In Medjugorje there is not much emphasis on healing. No one speaks about it very often or insistently. Prayers for healing are included in the hour after Mass when the glorious mysteries of the rosary are recited, as well as religious items being blessed. And that's about it for any formal prayers. However, informally in the hearts and minds of many pilgrims, prayers for healing of self, loved ones, and others are never far below the surface.

Medjugorje has not yet acquired the same reputation for healing as Lourdes, but it will quickly do so as the word spreads of what is happening there in that little Yugoslavian village. As I say, I was amazed at the number and scope of healings being reported.

The Parish Records

On Wednesday, June 6, 1990, I met with Father Slavko Barbaric who, like all the Franciscans of the parish, seems to do as much work each day as ordinary priests do on the most important holy days. Father Slavko has written the prayer book **Pray With the Heart** which contains a brief section on praying for healing. He is also in charge of recording healings which have been reported to the parish office. As of that date there were 363 healings which had been "accepted." This means that there was sufficient medical testimony presented to substantiate the healing. Father Slavko also added that, with the other cases now in progress, there would be about 400 healings in total very shortly. He mentioned that perhaps fifty of them had sufficient medical testimony to be declared "inexplicable by medical science."

A medical bureau has been established to investigate cases that have been reported to the parish, or which have been publicized in other ways. The bureau is in its infancy, but it is a good sign of growth and maturity in this important area. Lourdes has had a similar medical bureau which has become world famous.

At my meeting with Father Slavko I shared my intention to present cases of healing with which I was personally acquainted from my various pilgrimages to Medjugorje, as well as some of those which have been reported to the parish office.

From my personal experience (about twenty of my thirty years of priesthood have been devoted to the healing ministry, especially the last ten years as Director of the Sacred Heart Institute), I am convinced that healings take place all the time in big and little fashion. It has also been my experience that most healings are not instantaneous but happen gradually. Healing is most often a process, an evolutionary journey toward greater health and wholeness with many different stages.

Definitions and Divisions

Let's talk about some basic facts about healing before getting down to several cases.

We usually divide healing into four categories:

(a) physical healing;
(b) spiritual healing;
(c) emotional or inner healing; and
(d) deliverance, which is freeing a person from demonic influence of one sort or another.

Although we have this neat schema with its four parts, please understand that it is not always possible to be so neat and orderly. We humans are not noted for being terribly neat and orderly. Each category interacts with the others. Thus, a physical healing will have ramifications in both the spiritual and emotional life. Likewise, an emotional or spiritual healing will affect the other categories. And the devil will use any opening — physical, emotional, or spiritual — to try to do harm to us. So healing in any of the first three categories may free us from the power of evil (the fourth category).

Let us start with the healing that is the simplest to observe: the physical.

Stories abound of physical cures. They range from the earliest days of the apparitions (June 29, 1981) when Daniel Setka was cured to one of the more recent and best documented cases, Diana Basile.

Daniel had suffered from septicemia since the fourth day after his birth. He had multiple handicaps and had never spoken. His parents took him to Medjugorje and asked the visionaries to pray for the child. They agreed and said, "Dear Lady, is little Daniel going to speak some day? Cure him so that they will all believe us. These people love you very much, dear Lady. Perform a miracle. . . ." They repeated their petition and our Lady responded: "Have them believe strongly in his cure. Go in the peace of God."* That evening his healing was manifested when his parents stopped for something to eat and Daniel spoke his first words: "I'm hungry." In the next two months, he recovered completely.

Diana Basile

Diana Basile's cure is related, among other places, by Father Rene Laurentin in his book **The Messages and Teaching of**

*Father Rene Laurentin, **The Messages and Teaching of Medjugorje** (Milford, Ohio: Riehle Foundation, 1988).

Medjugorje and also in a talk he gave in the United States in October of 1989. Father Laurentin had visited Medjugorje twenty-eight times as of then and always checks with the parish office to see what healings have been reported.

Diana had been a victim of multiple sclerosis for twelve years, suffered motor difficulties in her arms and legs, and was blind in her right eye. In addition, she had acquired both urinary and fecal incontinence and suffered a skin disease as well. Her cure was instant when she went into the Apparition Room of the church on May 23, 1984. She was cured so completely that the next day she walked under her own power the ten kilometers from her hostel to climb the Hill of Apparitions.

Dr. Spaziante filed one hundred-fifty documents relating to her cure. These included results from tests more numerous and more modern than those which documented three recognized healings of multiple sclerosis at Lourdes.

As of June 1990, as I have mentioned, over three hundred-sixty cures have been reported to the parish office. Hundreds more have been documented but were not filed for one reason or another at the parish office in Medjugorje (Diana Basile being one of them).

My Own Experience

On one of the trips I took (February 1990), a woman was healed of a severe arthritic condition which had forced her to use a cane. She carried the cane for a few days after her healing as a precaution, but then gave it to another pilgrim.

Another woman from our area whom I knew well had a severe herniated disk condition which was quite painful. She experienced great pain on the trip over because of delays, etc. At Mass she always had to be in the back of the church on a special chair near the door in case she had to leave. At one Mass she went to the front of the church because her husband was with her and could carry her out if the pain became too much for her to bear. She experienced the gift of tears in abundance and felt extremely hot, so much so that she told her husband that she had to leave to get some fresh air. But she felt quite well. She thought she was just having a good day. Her healing was manifested when, on the next day, she was able to ascend and descend Mt. Krizevac without difficulty.

There are many other reports of physical healings which have occurred. A surgeon friend of mine was healed of a bad case of the flu while on Apparition Hill.

My own sister Elenore was healed of her diabetes for seven or eight weeks. She then had to go back on her medicine, but the doctor urged her not to lose faith in what had happened to her at Medjugorje. He told her that there are so many other serious complications with diabetes that she may have been healed of them. He also reassured her that our Lady, the medicine, and he himself would not let her down. What a beautiful sense he has of cooperating with God's plan for health and wholeness!

I have seen a video account of two healings that occurred in May 1989 when a film crew visited Medjugorje. A young woman, Patty, who was waiting for a heart and lung transplant, went to Medjugorje and was healed so that she was able to climb Mt. Krizevac. And a middle-aged Italian woman, suffering from multiple sclerosis, was healed in the village and was also able to climb the mountain and the Hill of Apparitions.

Vicka's Healing

One of the most impressive miracles of healing has to do with Vicka, the smiling, charming, gregarious visionary. She had an inoperable brain tumor and painful swelling of the joints. During several years Vicka was in great pain, and at times in a coma.

In February of 1988, Mary told her that she would be healed by Jesus on September 25 of that year. Vicka wrote letters to her confessor, the priests of the parish, and the Bishops' commission investigating the apparitions, telling them of our Lady's promise. She asked that the letters not be opened until September 26.

On the 25th of September she was healed as our Lady had promised. When the letters were opened, it was confirmed that our Lady had told her this in February. "It was a tremendous miracle with double grace: Vicka once again had her full health, and the commission had further proof of the authenticity of the apparitions, with records and documentation to corroborate Vicka's previous medical history."*

At a recent Medjugorje peace Mass one of the priests shared that on the plane to Medjugorje a woman showed him the documentation of a case of a young boy who had been healed there previously. The boy had been blind and deaf and was completely healed of those two difficulties. On the same pilgrimage, this priest also experienced a healing of another young man who had such poor eyesight that he was legally blind. He was healed on the mountain and was so confident in his new gift of sight that he walked down the mountain reading a book, which is no mean feat considering the condition of that mountain.

A Many-Splendored Thing

Another incident has the promise of a physical healing even as a spiritual one is occurring. This story touches me so deeply because it shows how God invites his people to reach out in healing love to one another.

A young man went to Medjugorje because his family was going and asked him to join them. He went because he loved his fam-

*Weible, p. 354.

A pilgrim climbs Apparition Hill

ily, but in no way did he believe. He had abandoned the Catholic faith several years before. In the group there was a seriously ill young woman who had been brought there by her parents. I had often prayed with her at Institute healing Masses, but she showed little improvement.

This young man was so touched by her courage that he designed and helped to build a sedan chair so that she could get to the top of Apparition Hill. It was quite a struggle for the young man and for the priest who was helping him carry the chair, but they made it to the top. On the way down, four Croatian teenagers took over and sped her down the hill. Now that was a miracle of sorts or at least the poor exhausted priest sees it that way.

An even greater miracle occurred in the young man's heart. He was so touched by the faith of the young lady and those around him that he turned back to the Lord. He received the sacraments and returned to the practice of his faith. Now that was spiritual healing, but it definitely had other overtones as well.

A Promise of More

By the way, the young woman with the serious disease who had to be carried up and down the hill believes that she will be healed. Her parents and many other people confirm that sense. In fact, it's been confirmed in so many ways that it's impossible to think they are just coincidental. She's been told that she will get worse before she gets better, but that eventually she **will** get better. This is an extreme case of what I mean by healing being a process. Please, begin to pray for her and be faithful in prayer because you may have a decisive part to play in her healing. That's not to induce a guilt trip; it's just a challenge and an invitation to you to be part of her healing.

Physical healings at Medjugorje are not scarce, but I would say that the majority of cases there involve emotional or spiritual healing. The previous story about the young man's conversion has many dimensions. It was an emotional and spiritual healing for him and in a different way and degree for the young woman who was so ill.

Emotional Healing

Emotional healing is also called healing of memories, or "inner" healing. Negative emotions can and often do cripple us. They can tie us up in such knots that we are unable to love ourselves, and consequently not able to love God or others. Jesus told us to love God with all we have and our neighbor **as ourselves.** All the rest is obviously impossible if we do not love ourselves.

Resentments and jealousy often prevent us from being able to forgive ourselves and others. Feelings of being unloved come from many sources, but their effect is devastating no matter what their origin. One of the great gifts of Medjugorje is peace. Our Lady has identified herself as the Queen of Peace. In my own experience of Medjugorje I've seen her give the gifts of peace and emotional healing in two remarkable instances.

Dying Well

In February of 1990, I went with nineteen other people to Medjugorje. Two of them have died as of this writing (July 1990). Both were healed emotionally and given the great gift of acceptance and peace. The man died first (May 22, 1990). He had left the United States to go back to his homeland in the Philippines to be with his family. He died surrounded by the love and great peace he had begun to feel so deeply in Medjugorje. The woman died in June and was also surrounded by her family. Peace came to her not in Medjugorje, but afterwards and very slowly. In the village and on her return, she questioned why others were healed and she was not. It was the concerted effort of her family and friends (including some of the February pilgrims) which helped her to walk through her doubts to her final peace. She, too, died thanking God for his love shown to her through so many people.

Living Well

A less dramatic but, in my mind, very startling healing of emotions occurred on our April pilgrimage. A group of seventy-six people was torn asunder by anger over accommodations. Half the group received the accommodation promised, while the other half were put in much more primitive surroundings. The contrast was stark indeed. There was anger, resentment, and a feeling of injustice, and obviously not a great deal of peace. Slowly, but surely, as I mentioned previously, a healing miracle occurred. The miracle was the gift of peace which is the fruit of Medjugorje in so many hearts. Slowly but surely, as people entered into the spirit of the daily Masses and rosaries and were exposed to the message of Medjugorje as well as the places of pilgrimage, a healing balm poured upon their hurt feelings. Our Lady was extracting the poison from the whole situation in her own gentle and loving manner.

Spiritual Healing

Spiritual healing is obtaining freedom from our sins and the consequences of those sins in our lives. It is conversion at a deep level of our being.

The spiritual healings which take place at Medjugorje are numerous because our Lady's urgent request for people to go to confession is a spur to hundreds, even thousands, of pilgrims each day. They literally line up and wait patiently to celebrate this great sacrament of healing, to be free of their sins and the remnants and consequences of those sins in their lives. People who have been away from the Church and the sacraments for ten, twenty, thirty-five, forty-five or even fifty-five years have received deep spiritual healing as they celebrated the sacrament of Penance, Reconciliation and Peace.

Archbishop Franic, recently retired leader of the Archdiocese of Split-Markarska in Yugoslavia, has urged his neighbor Bishop

Zanic of Mostar (who is opposed to the apparitions) to go to Medjugorje. He wrote, ". . . please go sometime, maybe even incognito . . . and begin to hear the confessions of the pilgrims. In this way, I am certain that you can best get to know Medjugorje — by seeing the miraculous conversion of souls, the greatest miracles which are happening in Medjugorje, in far greater numbers and in far greater intensity than in any other parish in Herzogovina and even in Lourdes." (An open letter from Archbishop Franic, made available to Catholic News Service in Washington, D.C., May 23, 1990.)

Our Lady has a definite program for spiritual healing which she asks us, ever so gently and urgently, to follow. She speaks often and consistently about the need for conversion and greater commitment to God. She calls for prayer, fasting, the sacraments — especially Mass and Communion and Confession. That's a beautiful way to be healed in any of the three categories we have mentioned, and also in the fourth one.

Deliverance

"And don't let Satan discourage you. He is working hard in the world" (January 14, 1985).

The devil most often tempts and attacks us from the outside (oppression). At times the devil may worm his way into the person in some way (obsession). An entirely different and much rarer occurrence happens when the devil manages in some manner to take over the individual's personality (possession).

If we think of a human being as a walled city, it helps to explain the three ways the devil influences us. Oppression is an attack upon us by the devil from outside the walls. We most often call this temptation. Obsession occurs when the devil has penetrated the wall in some way and has control over one part of us, but we are still free and fighting him. Possession means that the devil is in some way in control of the city.

The second category, obsession, has the devil influencing us because there is a hook or opening which allows him to work his mischief. This could be a physical, emotional, or spiritual illness which has weakened our defenses in some way.

When a person is healed, the devil no longer has the hook or opening and cannot influence the person. So we see how a physical, emotional or spiritual healing can deliver us from evil.

When tempted by the world, the flesh, or the devil, we call upon the help of God, Mary, and the angels and saints.

Our Lady continuously warns us to resist the attacks of the devil. She says, "Prayer is the answer, especially the rosary."

The Message of Hope

The category of deliverance frightens many people. Our Lady's message is clear and urgent, but she does not want to frighten us. Rather she wants to give us hope and courage. She has given us a spiritual program which will protect us.

Please, be aware of how much we all need to commit ourselves seriously and sincerely to that program. I would recommend that you be aware of the fact that the devil can attack you anywhere: in Medjugorje or on your return home. A good response is to pray daily for deliverance.

Pray the Our Father often and learn the prayer which follows it at Mass: "Deliver us, Lord, from every evil and grant us peace in our day. In your mercy keep us free from sin and protect us from all anxiety as we wait in joyful hope for the coming of our Savior, Jesus Christ. For the kingdom, the power, and the glory are yours, now and for ever." That last sentence is a powerful prayer and one we can use at any time of day or night no matter where we are.

Try to get to Mass and Communion often and even daily if you can. Spend some time in quiet adoration of the Blessed Sacrament. If the church is locked, sit in your car or walk up and down with that intention in mind. Or wherever you are, face in the direction of the nearest church and spiritually come into the presence of the Lord in the Eucharist.

Also remember that you, by Baptism and all the other sacraments, are the dwelling place of God, the Holy Trinity, Father, Son, and Holy Spirit. You are definitely a temple of God, so be aware of his presence and love. And ask the Blessed Mother to pray with you and for you that you will be able to receive God's promise and gift of love.

Our Lady's Words

Our Lady has spoken about healing, as the cure of the sick.

"For the cure of the sick, it is important to say the following prayers: the Creed, and seven times each the Lord's Prayer, the Hail Mary, and the Glory Be, and to fast on bread and water. It is good to impose one's hands on the sick and to pray. It is good to anoint the sick with holy oil. All priests do not have the gift of healing. In order to receive this gift, the priest must pray with perseverance and believe firmly" (7/25/82).

I believe every priest by his ordination is called to be a minister of healing, but that most of us have not realized or utilized this gift. In fact, in my book **Overcoming Obstacles to Healing,** I mention that every baptized Christian is called to be on the Lord's healing team. We — all of us — have a role to play in healing, but only and always under the Lordship of Jesus Christ. He is the healer and we are on his team, each called to share in this ministry according to our gifts and insights. Our Lady's call to priests "to pray with perseverance and [to] believe firmly" is good advice for them and for all God's people.

Healing Mass and Service

On my first pilgrimage to Medjugorje I was principal celebrant at the English Mass and did lead a gentle prayer for healing after Communion. Several people felt the need for more as is so often the case. Consequently, I agreed to have a healing service at 4:00 that afternoon at the still unfinished rotunda behind the Church of St. James.

While praying about the format for the healing service, I decided to use the one from Father Slavko's book **Pray With the Heart.** I wanted to be in union with the spirit of Medjugorje and to follow our Lady's messages for and about healing. We added some prayers of our own and some pilgrims from Hawaii sang that beautiful song to our Lady with which we began this book. It was all quite simple and prayerful and there was a definite peace surrounding and resulting from the service.

After we had finished the service, a few of us stayed to pray with a young man who felt under attack from the evil one. Sister Ruthann has already mentioned this incident and what it meant to her. There were some people from Italy, Hawaii, and Long Island who joined our group. It was a community of faith in the spirit of Medjugorje where all nations come together in and for peace. I sensed a tremendous power as the group of us prayed, and a real conviction that the young man was being healed in many areas of his life.

There are signs and wonders at Medjugorje which astonish people and the various healings are certainly in that category. Yet, as our Lady points out, they are done just so that people will believe the messages, convert and reform their lives, and live the messages no matter what the cost. Our Lady is aware of the devil's plans and attacks; and she warns us that our best defense is God's plan of five steps:

1. prayer;
2. fasting;
3. Scripture reading daily;
4. confession; and
5. Holy Communion.

* * * * * *

Why Not?

Why are some healed and others not at Medjugorje? or at Lourdes? or Fatima? or at healing Masses? or through the ministry of the Sacred Heart Institute?

Here are two viewpoints (not incompatible, we hope) which may help you in your efforts to sort things out in your mind.

* * * * * *

I (Father Ruane) remind you of certain things which I have learned over the years.

Jesus is the Healer. We who are baptized are called to be part of his team. Mary is definitely the ''star'' of his team, but always in submission to him.

Jesus heals in many ways and at various levels of our being. He may be healing our spirits, our attitudes and emotions, if not our bodies. The latter is always the easiest to grasp, but is not always the most important for our salvation.

Jesus is healing us now as we write and in the now of your reading. We need to be open to his healing light and touch, and that is not always easy for us who are often distracted by so many things.

Please, read and then join in saying this beautiful prayer which has helped me and others with whom I have shared it.

"Spirit of the Healing God, come and live in me. Touch me, calm me, and heal me. Love me into new and deeper life in and with Jesus and our loving Mother Mary."

Amen.

My Own Story

May I share a personal experience which may flesh out what I have said?

On my third pilgrimage to Medjugorje my allergies acted up rather strongly and caused or accompanied a case of bronchitis. It was a cross which, like many crosses, turned out to be a blessing in disguise. I do not enjoy being sick. A day or two of rest might be fine, but then I want to be up and out again. However, this bronchitis had a life and mind of its own, especially when mixed with nasal congestion and an allergic reaction. Needless to say, I did not recover in a hurry.

When I got home I had two days to rest up and then I began a series of healing Masses which necessitated my celebrating a healing Mass each day for four straight days. The Lord blessed the people who came to the Masses and me also. However, I was coughing so much as I prayed with people individually after Mass that many of them were moved to tell me, "I'm going to say a special prayer that you get better." I needed every prayer I received and was glad to get them. Besides, all of us, myself in particular, need the healing love of Jesus in our lives and the prayers of our brothers and sisters are vital for bringing that love to us.

But why wasn't I healed in Medjugorje? I didn't ask, as dumb as that may seem. I did, however, ask the Lord to get me home safe and sound and to help me to get better so I could celebrate the healing Masses. I didn't ask to be healed completely and Jesus didn't do it because there were lessons he wanted me to relearn.

Hidden Blessings

My illness did force me to curtail my schedule and to rest. That gave me time to reflect and journal about what God was saying to me through his Mother's appearances. I probably would not have done that if I had not been ill. God was quite willing to hit me over the head (or in the chest) to get my attention. He knows me well enough to know that I get so easily absorbed in what is going on at the moment that I tend to miss his word to me. I so often let the urgent get in the way of the important! I do it despite the fact that I urge other people to avoid it. That's one of the lessons the Lord wanted me to relearn. I hope I have gotten it right this time around.

Some people are healed physically at Medjugorje; many others are not. Why, I will never know; but since God is the Healer, he obviously has his reasons. We need to do all we can to accept and share his healings, but only God heals, so in the long run it's his responsibility.

* * * * * *

Another Perspective

Why some people are healed and others are not healed at Medjugorje or Lourdes or Fatima or wherever seems to me (Sister Ruthann) to be a question perhaps for God. Or maybe it shouldn't be a question at all, for who are we to demand explanations from God? Granted, he is our loving Father. But I can remember my loving earthly father occasionally responding to my "why?" with: "Because I said so, that's why."

However, I am as little satisfied with "just because" now as I was then. So maybe it's just that it isn't a question for God. Maybe it's a question each of us can only ask ourselves. Why aren't we always healed? Why wasn't I healed? Or was I? I would like to propose a two-part answer to this self-questioning.

Perhaps I Was Healed

The second part is the easier to bear and really relates to what Father has already said. That is, perhaps I **was** healed in a more important way than the way I wanted. Jesus himself proposed a question like that: "Which one of you would hand his child a stone when he asks for a loaf of bread, or a snake when she asks for a fish? If you, then, who are wicked, know how to give good gifts to your children, how much more will your heavenly Father give good things to those who ask him" (Matthew 7:9-11).

I think sometimes we ask for stones and snakes without realizing it. Not that I think physical illness or pain is "good." I don't. But if I had to choose for myself, I would ask for the healing of my soul above all else. My experiences in Medjugorje and post-Medjugorje are that this type of healing is never denied to those who ask for it. And sometimes it is given in preference to a physical healing. The soul, the spirit, is made well. What greater healing can we ask?

Do We Believe?

The first part of my answer to the question "Why wasn't I healed?" is more difficult to accept. But I think it is worth pondering and taking to prayer. I think sometimes, many times, we are not healed as we desire because we do not believe.

Not believe? Of course, I believe! And isn't that a rather strange thing for a Roman Catholic sister to say? And yet I, a Roman Catholic sister, do not believe, at least not enough. Lord Jesus Christ, help my unbelief.

When Jesus walked the earth, he healed . . . everyone and anyone who asked. Not once in the Gospels do I recall his saying, "No, I won't heal your leprosy, hemorrhage, blindness, paralysis because it's better for you than good health." What I do recall him saying, however, is "Your faith has healed you." And in Mark 6:6 we have the story of Jesus nearly unable to perform cures because of the "lack of faith."

Now before I go any further and before you start blaming yourself for any disease you might have that has not been cured, I need to say some other things. Because faith is a lot like passions: it comes in different sizes and shapes and intensities and densities or whatever. And, as we were taught, **it is a gift.** It is a pure and holy gift from God. Ask for it . . . ask for it every day, several times a day. Be like that importunate widow who pestered the judge so often that he finally gave in to her wishes (Luke 18:1-8). Or like the man who pleaded so persistently for bread from a neighbor who had already gone to bed that the friend finally relented, got up, and did as he asked (Luke 11:5-8). If we ask, we will receive.

It is important to remember, too, that because we are humans, living in a particular time in history, our faith — like everything else about us — is **culturally conditioned.**

Most of you who read this, as I who write it, are middle-class Americans of the latter half of the twentieth century, about to be dumped into the twenty-first. We have been born, raised, educated, and "televisioned" into the faith of our time and culture: faith in science and knowledge. Nor do I mean to suggest that science and knowledge are bad things. Far from it. But to put all our faith in them is a bad thing because it erodes, as it has eroded for centuries, our faith in the only One who can and does really take care of us.

History of Healing

I recently had to research the history of healing in the Church for a master's thesis. What I learned was very sad . . . and very hopeful. In the early days of the Church there were wonderful cures of almost every conceivable ailment. But as centuries passed, as we moved more and more away from the vitality and absolute commitment of that early faith, healings dwindled, faded away, became occasional moments instead of continuous days. And as we have placed our faith in science, in reason, in armaments, in our own capabilities, we have weakened our faith in God and his power to heal. And the point is that without total faith — on the part of somebody — healing doesn't happen. We must believe. But, the truth is, so often we don't, not really.

The summer before my pilgrimage to Medjugorje I had a bad fall and broke my right hand in several places. It wasn't set properly and so it didn't heal correctly. As it became obvious that two fingers were going to be crooked, I did pray. But I did not really pray for complete healing. I prayed only that my hand would heal enough that I would still be able to type. That's exactly what I got.

My Own Healing

As I prepared to leave for Medjugorje someone suggested to me that perhaps my hand would be completely healed there. Well, first of all, remember my private mindset at the time: I didn't believe in the apparitions. But even beyond that, I started making excuses for not being healed before I ever got near Yugoslavia. I remember quite clearly saying to the person, "Well, my hand is not so important. Maybe there's a limit on the number of miracles that can happen in a certain length of time. In that case, I think there are more important things in need of healing than my hand." What arrogance! I was making excuses for God! Lord, forgive me. Lord, help my unbelief.

Oh, I, as you, may believe that God **can** heal us. But that's a very different thing from believing that God **will** heal us. At least as far as physical healing is concerned.

I guess it's not so strange in this era of psychiatry, depth-psychology, 12-step programs, and I'm okay/you're okay, that we seem to have little trouble believing in inner healing (emotional, psychological, spiritual). We expect that through prayer, spiritual direction, and just a bit of therapy our psychic wounds can be healed. And very often that's exactly what happens. At least, those wounds are usually healed enough that we can get on about the business of "normal" living.

But ask yourself (as I ask myself), when you've got a broken bone, a bad case of flu, a heart ailment, cancer or whatever, if you expect to get well with prayer, spiritual direction, and just a bit of medicine. Even more dramatic, do you believe you will get well with "just" prayer? Do we **believe** we will be healed? Or do we just hope for it? There is a world of difference between them.

So why are some healed and others "not" healed? As I said before, my tentative answer is twofold. First, we need to take an honest look at our own "before and after." Have we been healed in some deep emotional or spiritual way? The answer is probably "yes." Then thank God for that great gift and ask yourself, if more healing is needed, do I believe that I will be healed? And pray for faith.

Let us all pray for faith. Let us pray for absolute faith. It is a gift from God and I do not believe he would deny it to us. Stand before our most loving Father, stand at the side of our Lady of Medjugorje asking her intercession, and pray for the faith that Jesus said could move mountains. As the gift is given and accepted, the healing will come.

And that I absolutely believe.

CHAPTER 14

Other Signs and Wonders

Many signs and wonders happen in Medjugorje and with religious items which are brought back from there. This has, as you might have guessed, caused quite a bit of excitement. In the early days of the apparitions the word "Mir," the Croatian word for peace, appeared in huge letters in the sky. And at times the cross of Krizevac disappeared to be replaced by a figure of a lady or a great light. People have taken pictures in Medjugorje which, when developed at home, revealed the luminous figure of a woman quite close to them. One of these photographs is on the cover of Wayne Weible's book.

I (Father Ruane) have seen pictures which were very convincing. One that touched me was of a woman at Apparition Hill. When the picture was developed, it showed a luminous, very beautiful feminine figure standing right near the woman, not facing her and not shoulder to shoulder, but in such a way that they were close enough to share, but not so close as to obstruct the view of the cross.

I've meditated on that scene as it speaks to me of Mary's role: to be close to us but never to block our view of her Son and his cross of victory over sin and death. In fact, she stands close enough to us that together we can gaze with love at her God and our God, her Savior and our Savior, at her Son and our brother.

Open Your Eyes

One young adult cried because she had not seen the "miracle of the sun" which so many pilgrims have reported seeing. The priest who was spiritual director with her group helped her to realize that seeing that miracle was not that important and that she needed to focus on the essentials (the messages and especially Mary's five-point plan). As the young woman was leaving, the priest asked how often she had been looking at the sun. She replied, "Oh, I don't do that. I'm afraid of hurting my eyes." He gently suggested to her that she would never see unless she opened her eyes.

Later on, she did see the miracle with open eyes. However, she also saw in another dimension how the priest was right about focusing on the messages and their application to our daily lives, not concentrating on secondary things.

Many people in Medjugorje have had their rosaries change from silver to gold. On my second trip I bought a rosary there. Slowly but surely as I used it and as I was preparing for my third trip, the rosary changed. Some links, parts of the medal, and the crucifix became golden. This has happened to me several times as I often give my rosary to people who seem to need an extra boost. As I start to pray with a new rosary, the links often change color not instantaneously but gradually. By the way, I've had to replenish my supply each time I've gone on pilgrimage.

Encouragement to Live the Messages

But what do these signs and wonders say? Our Lady has already told us that they are to prove the reality of what she is doing and saying. They are to encourage us to live the messages. They are not there as "brownie" points for us. They are there as incentives. Every time I pick up my rosary and I see that the links have changed from silver to golden, I am thrilled, but also reminded of how far I have to go to live the message.

The medal and crucifix of my rosary which are not completely changed inspire me to a greater commitment to praying the rosary. Not as a way to bribe our Lady to change it to gold, believe me. I'm sure the Lord and she know what I need and don't have to be "bribed" to give it to me. I still have a long way to go in becoming the human being, the Christian, the priest, the gentle person that the Lord wants me to be. My trust is in the Lord's love and his Mother's intercession, not in signs and wonders.

I Hope They Change

One woman was given two rosaries at separate times by priests who had been to Medjugorje, and the links on both rosaries changed from silver to gold. One of those priests was myself, and I know the rosary was silver when I brought it back. When she showed it to me later, it was certainly a golden hue. Being a little bit of a skeptic I wasn't completely convinced until another rosary, which I had given to someone else, also changed.

When I gave it to that person, she said, "Oh, I hope they change!" I gave her my usual comments on keeping one's gaze on the essentials of our Lady's message and she agreed, but then added, "I still hope they change."

What about that? Is it all right to hope that the links of your rosary will change to a golden color? I think so, as long as that is not the primary hope of your life. Why do some people receive this gift and others not? I don't actually know. I have some theories, though. First of all, perhaps those of us who experience this phenomenon need a little boost to our faith. Or perhaps, when a rosary is put aside and stays silver, it is a heavenly invitation to start using it. More than once this has caused the rosary links to turn.

One possible explanation for the phenomenon has been proposed by Rev. John Szantyr of the Diocese of Worcester, Mas-

A pilgrim prays at the beautiful statue in the plaza in front of the church. A white cross seems to appear in the sky behind the statue.

sachusetts. Fr. Szantyr was puzzled about the reported phenomenon of rosaries turning to gold, wondering what purpose there was. He took his question to prayer.

"During my prayer, these words came to me: 'As in the furnace he proved them.' I searched Scripture for these words and found them in Wisdom 3:5-6. 'Chastised a little, they shall be greatly blessed because God tried them and found them worthy of himself. As gold in the furnace he proved them.' I received my answer! With reflection and inspiration from the Holy Spirit, I adapted this teaching to the phenomenon of 'golden rosaries.'

"When gold ore is mined it comes from the earth unrefined and impure. The gold must be separated from the foreign elements clinging to it. In order to do this, the gold ore must pass through a hot furnace where the impurities are burned away leaving in the end pure gold.

"The scriptural text from the book of Wisdom likens us to gold. Due to original sin and its effects, we are weak in nature and prone to sin and faults of self-will. The human soul, that golden nugget which has been mined from the earth of sinfulness through the loving act of Christ's redemption, realized in the sacrament of Baptism, brought to salvation through the merciful love of the Divine Gold Miner (God the Father), needs to enter a purifying transformation.

"How does a soul arrive at this kind of purification? God sees the foreign impurities of sin and self-will still lining the gold nugget of our soul. He wants us to be pure gold, worthy of himself, holy and perfect as he is in himself. 'As gold in the furnace he tried them.' This means we must all pass through a spiritual furnace of the fire of God's love in order to be purified.

"Conversion is the beginning of the refining process of that gold nugget we call 'soul.' We enter into purification as we decide to enter into a conversion of life, to turn away from sin and anything related to sin. . . .

"In summary, what is this prodigy telling us? A change taking place on our rosaries is a call to personal conversion, to personal purification of our souls by the acceptance of each trial in our daily lives which represents that 'furnace of fire' making us holy. If God has blessed any one of us with this sign, his purpose is not to initiate boasting, entertainment, or hysterical wonder. It is simply a personal message given to each of us to respond to his call to be holy and worthy of the great plans he has in store for us in the future to bring us to happiness and peace.

"My rosaries turned a gold color recently [February 1988]. I suddenly found myself entering a new period of unexpected trials. I am reminded that my purification is for my greater holiness. My deeper prayer life will sustain me to the end."

— Rev. John Szantyr

Bless Them All

Many people bring back religious items which they have had blessed in Medjugorje. Before leaving Medjugorje, the bus and all the luggage loaded, I bless everything that everyone in our group has bought, wherever it is on their person, in their bags, or in the luggage compartment. Many of the items may have also been blessed after one of the Masses because that is a practice at Saint James. I make a very special point to bless everything **in** Medjugorje. Then I urge our pilgrims to give these religious items accompanied by some words about the messages and their meaning for our lives.

It's interesting how people always want to know if the objects have been blessed. How beautiful that people want their religious items blessed and consecrated to God. There is in all of us a deep yearning to be connected with God. Religious items are one way of establishing that connection. Our Lady has said that she wants us to have religious objects in our homes and on our persons. They are a great protection against the evil one and his machinations. Even more so, religious items proclaim who we are and Whose we are.

Just one final note on this subject. Some pilgrims have reported seeing some signs and wonders on returning to their homes. I surely am one of them as none of my rosaries has changed colors in Medjugorje, but only when I have **used** them at home. No matter where these phenomena occur, the guidelines we have just proposed are the same and will help us maintain the proper balance.

* * * * * *

I (Sister Ruthann), the great unbeliever, had a great deal of difficulty accepting the idea that rosary chains, medals and crucifixes changed from silver to gold. I mean, it seemed like some sort of magic trick and I wondered what possible reason God could have for "wasting" his time on tricks.

Even after I came to believe in our Lady's apparitions, I just couldn't get into the rosary-changing thing. And I privately thought that perhaps the metal used to make the rosaries sold in Medjugorje had some sort of interaction with body chemistry, causing them to take on a golden hue. Ah, science. Ah, knowledge.

When I went to Medjugorje, I took with me a rosary that I have had for many years. It was given to me by an elderly woman for whom I had a great love, and it was really my love for her that kept that rosary in my pocket. The point is that that particular rosary, which sits in my pocket at this moment, is gold, has always been gold, and — I assume — will continue to be gold. (Will I be the one whose rosary turns from gold to silver?) However, long years of use and non-use had dulled the finish, even worn it off in spots. So it was clear that the rosary had at one time been gold but was tarnished and not nearly so gold anymore.

A Delayed Reaction

In the months after my return from Medjugorje an amazing thing happened. The rosary became bright gold again even in places where it was most worn. At first I doubted the evidence of my own eyes. (Am I stubborn or what?) But finally I couldn't argue it away any longer. I showed the rosary to Father and he agreed with me that it had, indeed, become the golden rosary that it must have been fifty years ago.

I couldn't say it hadn't happened. But I could still wonder why. So I took my question to God and to the Blessed Mother. One day, while pondering the imponderable, I felt called to open my Bible. I did, at random, and my eyes fell on (believe it or not) Wisdom 3:5ff.

"Chastised a little, they shall be greatly blessed, because God tried them and found them worthy of himself. As gold in the furnace, he proved them, and as sacrificial offerings he took them to himself. In the time of their visitation they shall shine, and shall dart about as sparks through stubble."

Well, though our translations differ somewhat, both Father Szantyr and I were given the same reading. Of course, I didn't know that then. But when Father Ruane and I were working on this chapter and he handed me the piece Father Szantyr had written, I almost — but not quite — couldn't believe it! Our readings and God's teaching to us had been the same. How wonderful is our God!

But whether or not your rosary changes color, as Father Ruane has pointed out, is not the issue. Those of us who have experienced it probably needed it most. It is a boost to flagging faith and it is a source of strength in time of temptation. It is also a constant reminder of Mary's call to pray, pray the rosary — all fifteen decades — every day. And that prayer will lead us all to "dart about as sparks" of the Holy Spirit through "the stubble" of a wounded world.

CHAPTER 15

Vocations

We priests and religious, thank God, are not on the verge of becoming a vanishing species. However, there is definitely a vocation shortage in the Church of the United States and Western Europe. Priests and religious from Eastern Europe, Asia, and Africa are even now serving our local churches in the U.S. and Western Europe. Mother Theresa's Missionaries of Charity are just the most publicized part of the phenomenon of so-called mission churches sending out priests and religious to us.

Do our Lady's appearances at Medjugorje have something to say for the vocation shortage we are experiencing? I (Father Ruane) truly believe they do.

Vocations at or From Medjugorje

The Visionaries

Our Lady said to the visionaries: "I would like you to become priests and religious, but I leave you free to make your own choice."

Two of the visionaries, Ivanka and Mirjana, have married. They accepted our Lady's exquisite sense of respect for their freedom and they chose to marry.

Ivan did begin the process of joining the Franciscans, but did not continue those studies. He does not discuss such personal matters often but he has said that he might study psychology so as to be able to help families fulfill their roles. He is passionately interested in doing something about the breakdown of family life and sees psychology as a possible avenue for helping that situation. He should have an impact (possibly indirect) on vocations as he studies, speaks, and writes about families since they are cradles for sound vocations to the priesthood and religious life. He is the leader of one of the prayer groups in Medjugorje for young people, and I am sure some of them will decide to embrace the priestly or religious life.

Vicka and Maria may have a religious vocation, but they have not yet decided on their future. For now Vicka says she is doing what our Lady asks — meeting and teaching the pilgrims. She is ready to do whatever our Lady asks in the future.

Jacov is eighteen and he is a quiet, shy young man whom I sense may develop into a preacher and teacher. But for now he is very protective of his privacy. Since he was ten he has been the center of a storm of public attention. Consequently he never really had a normal adolescence and deserves to have his wishes for privacy respected. I pray for him often because the Lord has placed a special affection in my heart for him. I pray for the others also. They are a special group of young people, chosen by God and his Blessed Mother to be the means of spreading the Good News of the heavenly peace plan. What they do with their lives will be molded and formed by their daily contact with our Lady for so many years. Please join me in praying daily for them that they may continue to live the messages of our Lady.

Others Called at Medjugorje

In my few times at Medjugorje I have met and prayed with several groups of young adults who have heard the call to follow Christ as a priest or religious at Medjugorje.

Four young American men began the process of joining the Franciscan Province of the Assumption whose members serve at Medjugorje. These Americans are learning the Serbo-Croatian language right now.

A group of Italians whom I met on my first trip and with whom we had the healing service behind the church in the unfinished rotunda has kept in contact. One woman of the group, its natural leader, has been instrumental in helping twelve young men and several young women decide to begin their studies for the priesthood and religious life.

The young Italian man with whom Sister Ruthann and I and several others prayed in November of 1989 has kept in touch with me, and in January 1991 he will begin his studies for the priesthood in Rome.

There are people from our many pilgrimage groups from New Jersey and the whole United States who think they may be called but are trying to discern how and when they will respond. Pray for them and for the many unknown people, young, middle-aged, and older, who have been touched by Medjugorje. As they renew their lives in the holiness and prayer of the Medjugorje experience, either they or others will answer the call to the religious life and/or priesthood.

Our Call to Help

But back to what we can do for vocations. One thing, of course, is to pray and fast for that intention. These are very powerful weapons the Lord has given to us and our Lady has certainly underlined their importance. We also need to respect the priests and sisters in our midst and to show young people that we do. Priests and religious are human indeed and with the normal share of weaknesses. But they have been accepted, blessed, broken, and given for God's service. To become and to do all that takes much prayer on their part surely, but also demands the help and prayers of many others. No man or woman can do it alone, but definitely needs the prayers and loving support of family, friends, parishioners, and others as well.

Furthermore, we are called, I believe, to talk about vocations to our family members and other young and not so young persons who may give signs of being candidates for or likely recipients of God's call.

Called by Name

There is a vocation awareness program entitled **Called by Name.** It begins with the priests of each parish of a diocese preaching (usually for three weekends) a homily about vocations. The priest discusses what the signs of a vocation are, the various types of ministries involved, and how God today seems to be calling older men and women as well as younger ones: people who have found their jobs and life-styles unsatisfying even though they are quite successful in the eyes of the world, and who are willing to give up everything to follow the Lord's call. In the program, parishioners are asked to submit names of those who show some signs of being eligible candidates.

Without doubt, each of us deserves the right to be free to answer the call she or he hears. Nonetheless, all of us also need to be free and courageous enough to bring up the subject for discussion. During my thirty years as a priest, I have always talked about vocations and with certain people have urged them to think about the priesthood and religious life. At times I may have pushed too hard, but I doubt very much if many people are guilty of that particular failing. We tend to bend over backwards to avoid the subject. There are times when a few words from one of us might be just what someone needs who is thinking about the subject, but who isn't sure that he or she has what it takes. A word of encouragement is probably just what he/she needs to be confident enough to take the first step.

Perhaps we could take a lesson from our Lady's example. She told the children what she wanted and yet she respected their freedom to choose what vocation in life they felt called to live. Please recall the way she begins and ends her messages. Her requests highlight her exquisite sense of respect for our freedom.

"Dear children, I invite you to. . . . Thank you for hearing my call."

Let us invite young and not so young people to consider the call of the Lord. Older men and women, divorced as well, are eligible once their annulments have been received. Sister Ruth-ann will talk more about that later in this chapter.

The Eucharist and Vocations

I have recently read several articles which mention how Eucharistic adoration in a parish seems to be a great way to foster vocations. Killian McDonnell's article in **America** on that subject mentions the Emmanuel Community in France which has adoration frequently. That community is reported to have provided two-thirds of the vocations to the priesthood in France in recent years. Their leaders believe there is a definite correlation between the wealth of vocations and Eucharistic adoration. A recent issue of **Maryknoll** magazine comments on that same phenomenon in one of their mission parishes.

Eucharistic adoration is something which seems to be reviving in our Church and also reviving our Church in the process. In Medjugorje many pilgrims experience a tremendous hunger for a time and place to be quiet. There are always so many people and activities. In February I realized this more and more because I was free of most duties and yet the only place I could be alone was either in my room — luckily I had my own private room — or the cemetery. It is about a quarter mile behind the church and quite old and set in a clump of trees.

In the Church of Saint James in Medjugorje there are normally too many people for me to be able to get quiet. I have gone to Church in the early morning to meditate during the Croatian Mass, but that is not the best time or place. Usually it's only in my room and in the cemetery that I can be quiet.

Thank God the parish has recently built a chapel (attached to the new rectory) where there will be complete silence and adoration of the Blessed Sacrament for many hours each day. What a joy to satisfy that deep hunger so many people feel, and to do so in the presence of Jesus, in his Eucharistic presence. I foresee Medjugorje's not insignificant impact on vocations increasing dramatically as a result of such Eucharistic adoration on so sustained a basis.

My Prayer for Vocations

When I pray for vocations I pray for those of us who have been called to the priesthood and religious life that we may deepen our commitment to the Lord and his work. I am this year celebrating thirty years of priestly life. Much has changed in those thirty years and much will change in the next thirty years. My time before the Blessed Sacrament has sustained, energized, and renewed my priestly enthusiasm and zeal. My times in Medjugorje have always been centered around the Eucharist and the church, although I would never want to deny the tremendous renewal of priestly zeal and the fire of the Spirit I experienced on my first visit to Apparition Hill. You may remember how at that time I asked Jesus to relight the fire of my priestly zeal through the intercession of our Lady. When I pray for those who have already answered the call for five, ten, twenty-five, fifty or more years, I pray for a similar recharging of their batteries and for perseverance and a joy deeper than any anxiety or doubt which might assail them.

No matter what changes take place in our church, we will always need vocations to the priesthood and religious life. As our own Archbishop of Newark, New Jersey (Theodore E. McCarrick) has said so often, "The vocations are there and it's up to all Catholics, especially parents, to promote them." He has given all of us in the Archdiocese a great awareness of the need for vocations. It is one of his priorities as the shepherd of this local church of Newark, New Jersey. At his suggestion each week there is a Holy Hour for vocations in one of our over two hundred forty parishes. These are publicized in our Archdiocesan newspaper and I sincerely hope that readers whisper a prayer for vocations each time they see it even if they cannot attend. No one's prayers are unneeded or unwanted.

Let us ask God to really bless us with many vocations to the priesthood and religious life. We need also to pray for those who marry that they may live out the great sacrament of matrimony. Let us also pray for those who are single, either by choice or by circumstances, that God will bless them also with a great sense of his love. We must pray too for those whose lives are not yet determined, who are trying to decide about what they want to do with their lives. Let us pray that they will be guided not by what the world thinks but by what the Lord thinks and wants for them.

* * * * * *

My Own Vocation

Because we're talking about vocations, I (Sister Ruthann) would like to tell you a short story about my own vocation. Though it doesn't have to do specifically with Medjugorje, it does have to do with thinking about and praying for vocations. So I include it here.

I was thirty-seven when the idea first jolted through me that I might enter the convent. I had been married at eighteen, divorced at twenty-five, and had opted out of any thought of an annulment because I had absolutely no desire to marry again. I remember when I first met Father

Ruane in 1975 (I was teaching at Caldwell College where he was professor and campus minister), and as we got to know each other, he suggested more than once that I try to get an annulment. But I wasn't interested.

As years went by I began to feel restless, unsettled, despite a very successful career; and I thought seriously of moving back to Tennessee and accepting an excellent job in advertising that I'd been offered. In fact, I was making plans to do just that. But God intervened and let me know the plan **he** had in mind. I yielded. My restlessness disappeared.

Some might have called it mid-life crisis. I call it grace.

Annulment Needed!

Imagine my surprise when, having gathered enough courage to approach the Caldwell Dominicans' vocation director, I found out that I needed an annulment in order to enter! By now it was 1980 and I hadn't seen my ex-husband since 1968 so I expected a rather long and arduous struggle to find him and get all the paper work done. Well, when God wants something to happen, things move. I had my annulment in hand seven months after I started the process.

I was thirty-eight when I entered, an age when most of us are "settled" into our lives. And what I discovered was that I had indeed been "made new" in the Lord Jesus Christ. All the experiences I had had, the talents I had developed have been transformed in the hands of Jesus. Nothing was wasted, and everything was blessed into newness. Life became and continues to be an adventure in discovering myself, my gracious God, and the holiness of all life.

Of course, I hear a lot of comments about my being a "delayed vocation." Balderdash. Why shouldn't God call the older as well as the younger? What about Abraham and Sara, Zachary and Elizabeth? I believe that when I was ready and God was ready, he spoke a word deep within me. And he graced me with the insight and courage to say "yes" to him and "no" to everything else.

It's never too late. I know that. And sometimes I kind of smile to myself because I think that Jesus (who undeniably learned a lot from his wonderful Mother) whispers to me, "Thank you for hearing my call." I can only respond, "Thank you for calling."

On Apparition Hill

CHAPTER 16

The Beautiful Mosaic of Medjugorje

As we have said before when we began this book, we didn't realize the full extent of all that there is to be said about Medjugorje and the ways in which our Lady's messages can influence our lives. We could probably keep writing for years and not cover it all. So some topics fell by the wayside. We leave them for later.

But there were three subjects we felt needed to be included: witnessing to others of the impact Medjugorje has had on us; judging the apparitions by their fruits; and finally, friendships resulting from a common interest in what our Lady is saying and doing in Yugoslavia and throughout the world. All three of these subjects are too important to be excluded and too interrelated to be separated.

If we bring forth fruits worthy of our Lady's plan, we will be witnessing effectively to a world starving for that great gift of peace. Our friendships will give us the strength, nurturing, and monitoring which will lead us to the feet of our gracious Queen of Peace. That will be the most effective witnessing we can do and will bear the best fruit of all.

These last few thoughts are gathered together in the last chapter, but they are far from being postscripts. Rather, they are three small and particularly beautifully colored pieces in the glorious mosaic that is Medjugorje.

* * * * * *

WITNESSING

People really are interested in Medjugorje. The subject crops up at the most interesting times. I (Father Ruane) am surprised at how many people have heard about Medjugorje. (I'm also surprised at how many have not!) My feeling is that what sparks this interest is how the people who have been to Medjugorje or are interested in it have been touched by the messages and have decided to share the experience with friends and relatives.

There are various ways of sharing and my suggestion is always to do it very lovingly and with a great sense of peace. Never — repeat — never back anybody into a corner. Just share what happened to you. Many times the best thing to do is to let the message change you and to let this be so apparent in your life that people will say, "You're different; something has happened to you! What is it?" Then we have to be able to share what the message of Medjugorje is. Why not practice what you're going to say? Keep it simple and be peaceful. The outcome is God's concern, not yours. Share what's happened to you and do so in a way which is respectful of the other person's freedom.

I Invite You

Once again, I point to our Lady's modus operandi — manner of acting. She always says, "I invite you to pray with the heart, to pray for peace, to conversion, to fasting." She always concludes, "Thank you for hearing my call." What a beautiful, gentle, and gracious lady she is. No force, just a beautiful message. She repeats it often so that ears that may not have been able to hear the first time will hear it the second or third time. She gives us an example of how we are to act, to share, and to move in God's love.

May she teach us how to love others and to invite them to hear and answer her requests for conversion, faith, prayer, fasting, and for Mass and confession regularly. May she who is the

Queen of Peace grant us peace in abundance as we witness to her and share our convictions about Medjugorje.

* * * * * *

More Subtle Ways

There are other, subtle ways of witnessing too that I (Sister Ruthann) have found myself or been shown by friends of mine who have been to Medjugorje. I might add that I have been bullied into total rebellion by at least one person who was an early visitor to Medjugorje (when no one could even pronounce it, much less attempt to spell it). She came back insisting, demanding even, that I believe her story of our Lady's appearing in some backwater of Yugoslavia. Do I have to tell you what my reaction was? I thought she was a nut! Father is absolutely right when he says not to back anybody into a corner. Their most immediate and gut-level reaction is to fight, hardly the message of the Queen of Peace.

But I have found that wearing a Medjugorje medal will often begin a conversation, even in the most unlikely places, like gas stations and grocery stores as well as in the more "obvious" church vestibule. Some recognize the very distinctive figure of our Lady with her veil blowing in the wind. Lo and behold! I have found a new Medjugorje friend, whether or not that person has actually been there. Keeping to the Wednesday and Friday fast is another way. People are curious. They ask. And when they see our lives matching our words, they listen to our answers.

A Silent Witness and Gift of Love

And then there is my very dear woman friend who wears a most beautiful Medjugorje medal that is cut in the pattern of our Lady of Medjugorje (wind-blown veil, cloud, and all) rather than the usual square or oval shape. She and I were having lunch one day and I commented on how beautiful it was. She replied that this was her "Medjugorje ministry," that anyone who commented on it was obviously meant to have one. And with that, she reached into her purse, pulled one out, and gave it to me. She said that many, many people have noticed it, some of whom had never heard of Medjugorje. This ministry then gave her the opportunity to tell the story and to speak gently of the messages. What a witness my friend gives to all of us: believer and nonbeliever alike.

There are as many ways to witness as there are people to do the witnessing, and each of us will find his or her own way. I do feel, however, that the very best witness we can give is how we live, how we let the plan of Jesus and Mary overtake our lives and change them. Then, as Father says, people notice. They ask. They are eager for an answer. My prayer for all of us is that our answers will be as gentle as Mary's invitation and that she will then be able to say to us, "Thank you for hearing my call."

* * * * * *

JUDGE IT BY ITS FRUITS

The Holy Father was asked in June 1986 by twelve Italian bishops, about Medjugorje. They knew about his great devotion to the Blessed Virgin Mary. He is reported to have said, "If I were not Pope, I would go to Medjugorje myself." I (Father Ruane) believe he would because he loves to travel and especially loves to visit shrines of our Lady. The twelve Italian bishops obviously felt a need for his pastoral direction and probably sensed his great interest in anything to do with Mary. They explained that their people were going on pilgrimage there and returning home, having been converted, doing penance, praying and fasting. The Pope's reply was, "Let them go to Medjugorje if they are converting and doing penance, praying and fasting."

A village home in Medjugorje

The Holy Father was using a time-honored pastoral principle, ". . . you can tell a tree by its fruit" (Matthew 12:33). And a spiritual movement such as an apparition can be judged by its fruits also. What are the fruits of Medjugorje? Well, let's consider the Italian bishops' views. They saw that the fruits were the basic components of the Gospel message: commitment to the Lord, doing penance, praying, and fasting. The result of all this is the gift of peace, the same gift which the risen Savior gave his disciples at his resurrection appearances.

Peace and Renewal

I have seen similar fruits of peace and renewal in my various visits to Medjugorje. Many other priests have also. The number of priests from my own Archdiocese who have had similar experiences has amazed me. We often speak of how affirming of our priestly ministry a pilgrimage to Medjugorje is. We are renewed in our priestly dedication by sharing in the vibrant Eucharists, and by receiving ourselves the great sacrament of Penance/Reconciliation. Then we have the joy of hearing confessions with so many people from around the world, and finally to be bathed in the ocean of prayer and praise which occurs at Medjugorje.

Father Ken Roberts has shared his views many times. He once took sixty young adults there, forty-three of them young men. They ranged from the tepid to the fervent with more in the former category than the latter. By the time they left Medjugorje, they had experienced many deep and life-changing moments. Even Father Roberts, for all his retreat and mission work with young people, was utterly surprised and astonished by the spiritual renewal these young adults had undergone in just one short week.

A Traveller's Nightmare

Their return was a traveller's nightmare (a real horror story) including four hours of sitting in a plane at Zagreb in 100 degree heat and they had no air-conditioning. There were long delays at customs in the U.S., and missed connections for their domestic flights. Through it all, there was perfect peace and a constant praying of the rosary, singing of hymns and witnessing to one and all of what the Lord and his Mother had done in their lives.

In my eyes, that was a major miracle. I spent more than ten years of my priesthood working with young people and took groups of one hundred twenty and more of them to two national conferences. They were the cream of our young people, participants and leaders in our Archdiocesan youth programs. They were good people but, believe me, it took all the "DI" (Drill Instructor but sans vulgarities) in me to keep them in line and focused on "why" we were travelling, etc.

12:40 Club

Some of our pilgrims started a club while on the plane home. They agreed to pray for peace each day as close as possible to the time of the apparition (6:40 p.m. in Yugoslavia). They called their group the 12:40 Club. I hope they persevere because a little prayer each lunch time will never hurt any of us. And if the 12:40 Club catches on, then the waves of prayer flowing up to the Lord our God from Medjugorje at that time each day may be matched and mingled with those from all parts of the U.S. and the world.

Why not discuss the 12:40 Club idea with family, friends, co-workers, prayer partners? Timing isn't the important part of the idea although psychologically it certainly is a good reinforcement of one's zeal. What is important is to join in the prayers of so many people, to bring forth fruits of prayer, fasting, and conversion in our own lives which are worthy of the love bestowed on us by the Mother of God, our beautiful Queen of Peace.

FRIENDSHIPS

This section is obviously more pertinent to those who have travelled to Medjugorje, but not exclusively so. If you have an interest in Medjugorje, and you must if you've read this far, try to get to a Peace Mass in the spirit of Medjugorje or to one of the many prayer groups which are growing up all over the country. Once there, ask Jesus and his Mother to direct you to people with whom you can share.

There are centers all over the United States and other countries devoted to spreading the message of Medjugorje. Many diocesan newspapers carry ads or notices on pilgrimages to Medjugorje. Contact them as they should know where there is a group you can join. As a last resort, call us at the Sacred Heart Institute and we'll put you in contact with the group nearest you.

The friends you make on your pilgrimage are a blessing while there, but they are even more so at home. Value them as they are most helpful, especially if you get together for prayer and sharing while in Medjugorje and certainly when you return home.

One man who had been on pilgrimage with me reacted very strongly when I mentioned dropping this section from the book. He felt that he would never have gotten to know me and my family and vice versa if we had not stayed in touch.

There are many other people from the U.S. and all over the world whom I have met in Medjugorje. Some are special friends now because of our shared experiences. One of my three sisters has kept in close contact with the group who stayed in the same house with us on our April pilgrimage. They pray and talk together, exchange visits, books and videos. They nurture each other, pray for each other, and find solace, comfort, strength and encouragement to persevere when things get rough.

What It Means to Be a Pilgrim

Wayne Weible shares some insights on this subject. "I had a new understanding of what it meant to be a pilgrim — to share experiences and impressions with others from all different backgrounds who were placed with you for a period of time. . . . As soon as the seat belt sign was turned off, we gathered in little groups talking about our plans and arranging get-togethers when we got home."*

I suggest that you stay in contact, if at all possible, with the priest who was the spiritual director, with friends you made there, and with others in your neighborhood who have been to Medjugorje.

You'll need people to share with, so seek them out, and rather quickly. They will be a great outlet and you won't feel an unbearable pressure to talk too much with other people who need to be handled with kid gloves. There are two extremes to be avoided: one thinks nothing ever happened before your pilgrimage; the other is so afraid to offend anyone that he or she says nothing at all.

When you return, keep the memories green (a good AA slogan) because our Lady has repeatedly warned how the world, the flesh, and the devil are always on the lookout to snatch the good news and its power away from you as soon as possible. The best way to keep those memories alive and well is to join with others who are interested in Medjugorje whether they've been there or not, and do what our Lady asks — pray the rosary, participate at Mass, fast, and commit your life to God.

The next section will be helpful in suggesting ways to get friends of Medjugorje together.

*Weible, p. 135.

A woman of Medjugorje and her cow

The Medjugorje Dinner Party

A group of nine people — all of whom had been to Medjugorje — came together for a dinner party, but it was destined to be more than that.

It was held at the rectory where I'm in residence during my sabbatical. The pastor had another appointment, so I acted as host. One person brought a cake, someone brought wine, another brought candy; but everyone brought many other things too. They brought memories of Medjugorje. They brought the things that had touched them — pictures, rosaries, prayer books, and a desire and a need to talk and to share with people who had experienced it. One person even brought the latest book of the messages of Medjugorje.

That evening we shared food and lots of laughs. But we shared much more about what we had experienced at Medjugorje and what had been our Lady's message to each of us while in that beautiful little farming village in Yugoslavia.

People came from several areas, in fact from two states, just to be there. There was a beautiful openness and a real sense of being part of something very special and not wanting to keep it to oneself, but to share it with others. As I listened to what they were sharing and as I shared myself, I began to realize how well some people are appropriating the message of Medjugorje, how they are bringing it back to their families and communities and helping it to take root in their towns, parishes, and communities. What a cause for giving thanks to God!

Five of them had been to Medjugorje only once. Three had been there three times and one man had been there five times within a short length of time. He literally could not get enough of it and God had blessed him so that he was able to travel to Medjugorje for a week every two months or so. His wife was with us that night and she had gone with him three times and encouraged him to go the other two times.

We ate well but we were still hungry . . . for spiritual food, and we felt a real sense of gratitude to God for doing his special work in us through our Lady. One man mentioned that he was in Medjugorje only two days when he seemed to achieve a peace that he had never had before and which stayed with him throughout the rest of his time there. He, as so many others, had climbed Krizevac and spent quite a bit of time on the top away from the crowds and alone with the Lord. There many things became clear and his peace was deepened.

We all agreed that Medjugorje is a holy place, a place of prayer and peace where penance and fasting, the Eucharist and Reconciliation are a delight. My only regret about our evening together was that we did not spend more time in prayer, especially the rosary.

But there will be a next time. Then I'm sure that all of us will want to conclude our sharing about the messages and what they mean to us by responding in prayer to what our Lady is asking.

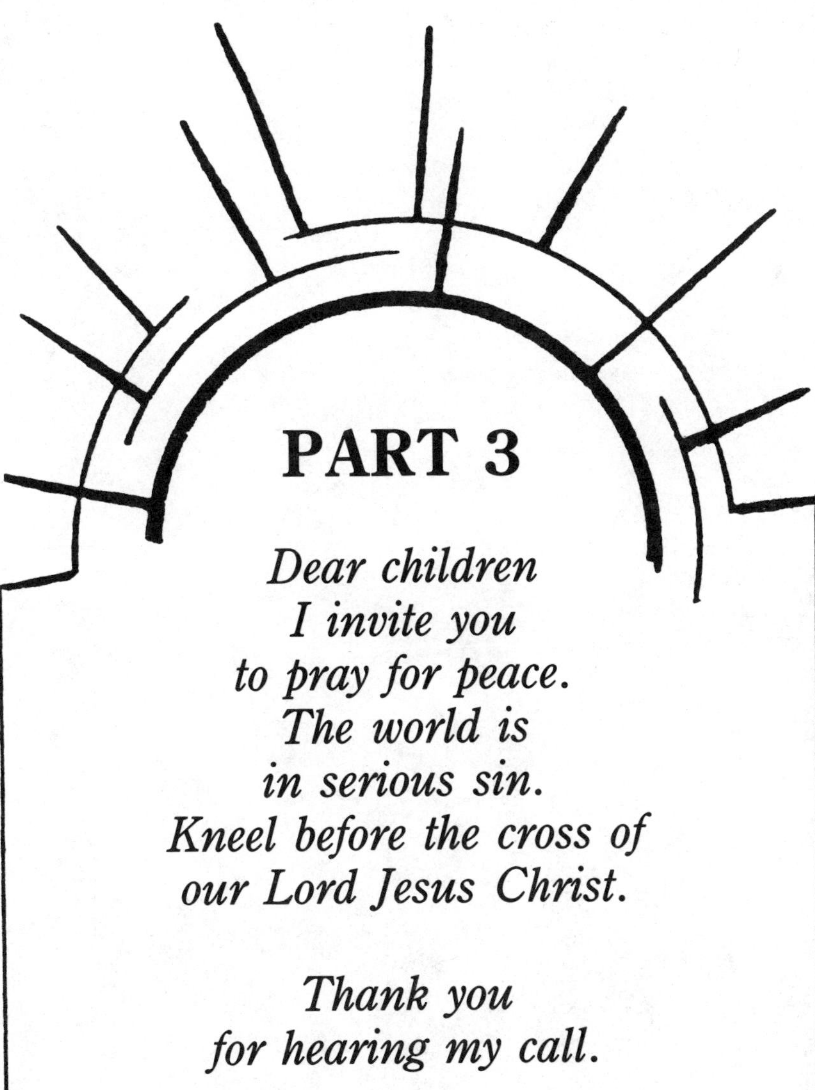

PART 3

Dear children
I invite you
to pray for peace.
The world is
in serious sin.
Kneel before the cross of
our Lord Jesus Christ.

Thank you
for hearing my call.

PART 3

Conclusion

As we come to the end of our written reflection, one truth is paramount. We are called to live the message of Medjugorje. We need to appropriate the healing grace of Medjugorje in our normal everyday lives. We hope and pray that what we have shared in this book will have helped. And yet the only one who can live the message in your skin and in your life, your home, your family, your town and parish community is, of course, you. You alone. Our Lady gave us her plan for peace in her messages. We alone can provide the postscript to those messages which verifies and validates their content.

Our prayer is that this book will have helped you to see some added possibilities for doing so. May you realize that all the songs of Medjugorje are not in Croatian and they are not all sung in Yugoslavia. Many of them are sung in our own country, in our own words, and perhaps even in our own keys. We sing them ourselves, and perhaps — like Frank Sinatra — we need to be able to sing "I did it my way" to the praise and glory of God and to the honor of his Blessed Mother. Those are the best songs, the ones we sing with our hearts and live with our lives.

And So We Pray

Let us now pray together.

Lord Jesus Christ, you became flesh and you lived among us so that we might be saved from our sinful ways and filled with the grace of your Holy Spirit. Bring us to a deeper realization of the fact that we are the beloved children of God, our heavenly Father. Enable us to stand on the truth which has been proclaimed in your name throughout the centuries by the holy Catholic Church. We claim the intercession of your Mother and all the saints and angels, the faithful on earth, and the souls in purgatory, so that we may know and do your will in our daily lives.

We believe that you have spoken once again in our time through your Blessed Mother. We believe that you have used her to touch many hearts beginning with the six visionaries in Medjugorje, then with that parish community and the neighboring towns, with the thirteen million and more pilgrims who have come there from every part of the world, and finally with the untold millions who have been touched by her message as it has spread around the world by an avalanche of books, audio and video tapes, newsletters, but especially by those who have dedicated themselves to being missionaries of your plan for the world peace presented to us by Mary, the Queen of Peace.

Let us hear your message clearly. Let us understand what you want us to know and to love and to do. You have made us for yourselves and our hearts are restless until they rest in you.

Through our Lady of Peace, our Lady of Medjugorje, help us to come into a peace and understanding, a quality of life and mind that will help us to rest in you and let our hearts focus on you. Amen.

A FINAL WORD FROM OUR LADY

We conclude with a final word from our Lady, the Queen of Peace, the cause of our joy and the best and most faithful disciple of Jesus our Lord.

Our Lady's Call

"Dear children! Today I call you to decide whether you want to live the messages I give you. I want you to be active in living

and conveying the messages. Especially, dear children, I want you all to be Jesus' reflection which will shine to this unbelieving world walking in darkness.

"I want you all to be the light to everyone and to testify in the light. Dear children, you are not called to darkness but to the light. Therefore, live the light with your life!

"Thank you for hearing my call" (June 5, 1986).

"Dear children, I have been inviting you for years by these messages which I am giving you. Little children, by means of the messages I wish to make a very beautiful mosaic in your heart so I may be able to present each one of you to God like the original image. Therefore, little children, I desire that your decisions be free before God, because he has given you freedom. Therefore, pray so that, free from any influence of Satan, you may decide only for God. I am praying for you before God, and I am seeking your surrender to God.

"Thank you for hearing my call" (November 25, 1989).

"Dear children, today I desire to invite you to take with seriousness and put into practice the messages which I am giving you. You know, little children, that I am with you and that I desire to lead you along the same path to heaven which is beautiful for those who discover it in prayer.

"Therefore, little children, do not forget that these messages which I am giving you have to be put into your everyday life in order that you might be able to say, 'There, I have taken the messages and try to live them.' Dear children, I am protecting you before the heavenly Father by my own prayers.

"Thank you for hearing my call" (August 25, 1990).

About the Authors

Rev. Gerald P. Ruane, Ph.D., is a Roman Catholic priest of the Archdiocese of Newark, New Jersey. He has been Director of the Sacred Heart Institute since its inception in 1979. Additionally, he served as pastor of Holy Trinity Church, Westfield, New Jersey, from November 1987 through September 1989, when he was given a sabbatical leave to study and write.

Father Ruane has a doctorate in religious education and has done graduate work at the Catholic University of Louvain, Belgium, and at Oxford University in England.

An internationally known writer, Father is the author of five previous books: **Daily Homilies for the Year** (1968), **Birth to Birth: The Life-Death Mystery** (1976), **Overcoming Obstacles to Healing** (1985), **Healing and Your Emotional Life** (1986), and **The Eucharist** (1989), which is volume 1 of a series "The Greatest Healing Gifts."

Father is a charter lifelong member of the Association of Christian Therapists.

Sister Ruthann Williams, O.P., is a member of the Dominican Sisters of Caldwell, New Jersey, and is the Administrator of the Sacred Heart Institute. She holds a master's degree from Drew University and is presently completing a second master's from Immaculate Conception Seminary, the major seminary of the Archdiocese of Newark, New Jersey.

In the last few years Sister has given retreats and days of recollection and healing in New Jersey, New York, Pennsylvania, California, and Massachusetts. She leads many days of healing of women and speaks frequently for groups of separated and divorced Catholics.

Her articles and poems have been published in regional and national magazines, most recently in **The Priest, Brothers,** and **Sisters Today.** An article which Sister coauthored on pastoral care for the sexually addicted has been translated into several languages for worldwide distribution.

Sister's first book, **Healing Your Grief,** was published in 1987; her second, **Go in Peace: Healing for Women,** in 1990.

Sister is a member of the Association of Christian Therapists.